New Directions for
Student Services

John H. Schuh
EDITOR-IN-CHIEF

Elizabeth J. Whitt
ASSOCIATE EDITOR

Developing Effective Programs and Services for College Men

Gar E. Kellom
EDITOR

Number 107 • Fall 2004
Jossey-Bass
San Francisco

DEVELOPING EFFECTIVE PROGRAMS AND SERVICES FOR COLLEGE MEN
Gar E. Kellom (ed.)
New Directions for Student Services, no. 107
John H. Schuh, Editor-in-Chief
Elizabeth J. Whitt, Associate Editor

NEW DIRECTIONS FOR STUDENT SERVICES (ISSN 0164-7970, e-ISSN 1536-0695) is part of The Jossey-Bass Higher and Adult Education Series and is published quarterly by Wiley Subscription Services, Inc., A Wiley Company, at Jossey-Bass, 989 Market Street, San Francisco, California 94103-1741. Periodicals Postage Paid at San Francisco, California, and at additional mailing offices. POSTMASTER: Send address changes to New Directions for Student Services, Jossey-Bass, 989 Market Street, San Francisco, California 94103-1741.

New Directions for Student Services is indexed in College Student Personnel Abstracts and Contents Pages in Education.

Microfilm copies of issues and articles are available in 16mm and 35mm, as well as microfiche in 105mm, through University Microfilms Inc., 300 North Zeeb Road, Ann Arbor, Michigan 48106-1346.

SUBSCRIPTIONS cost $75 for individuals and $170 for institutions, agencies, and libraries. See ordering information page at end of book.

EDITORIAL CORRESPONDENCE should be sent to the Editor-in-Chief, John H. Schuh, N 243 Lagomarcino Hall, Iowa State University, Ames, Iowa 50011

Jossey-Bass Web address: www.josseybass.com

CONTENTS

EDITOR'S NOTES   1
Gar E. Kellom

1. Reflecting on Reconnecting Males to Higher Education   9
Obie Clayton, Cynthia Lucas Hewitt, Eddie D. Gaffney
Morehouse College is playing a leadership role in the attempt to under-
stand recruitment, retention, and success issues for men.

2. Men's Studies as a Foundation for Student Development   23
Work with College Men
Rocco L. Capraro
Hobart and William Smith Colleges, with the only men's studies minor
in the country, provides insight on how to address men's issues both
inside and outside the classroom.

3. A Women's College Perspective on the Education of   35
College Men
Cynthia Neal Spence, Manju Parikh
Women's studies can not only be supportive of the efforts to educate
men on gender issues but also provide insight on how to do it effec-
tively.

4. Connecting Men to Academic and Student Affairs Programs   47
and Services
Tracy Davis, Jason A. Laker
By understanding barriers and opportunities, more effective programs
and services can be designed.

5. Best Practices for Improving College Men's Health   59
Will H. Courtenay
This chapter examines why college men's health risks are high, how
they learn unhealthy attitudes and behaviors, and evidence-based
strategies to improve men's health.

6. Arrested Emotional Development: Connecting College Men,   75
Emotions, and Misconduct
Randall B. Ludeman
By drawing on men's studies, student judicial systems can help men
better understand themselves and how they got there.

7. Men, Spirituality, and the Collegiate Experience   87
W. Merle Longwood, Mark W. Muesse, William C. Schipper, O.S.B.
Addressing spirituality and men's awareness of masculine ideals can
help enhance college men's lives.

AFTERWORD   97
Michael Kimmel

INDEX   101

EDITOR'S NOTES

We begin with some questions. Is there a problem with enrollment, retention, and academic performance of college men? What data do we have, and do they illustrate a pattern to be concerned about? Is the situation exacerbated at liberal arts colleges? If we think there is a problem, what do we, as higher education administrators, do about it? How might one focus on engaging men while not diminishing the positive and important momentum in the improvement of education for college women?

I originally wrote about this situation in a paper for the Oxford Round Table on Residential Colleges, recounting headlines that had been appearing such as "Where the Boys Aren't," "More Women Filling College Classrooms Than Ever Before," "Liberal Arts Colleges Ask: Where Have the Men Gone?" (Kellom, 1999). Articles continue to appear on the same subject ("How the B.A. Gap Widens the Chasm Between Men and Women," Hacker, 2003; "The New Gender Gap: From Kindergarten to Grad School, Boys Are Becoming the Second Sex," Conlin, 2003). One excerpt from the Conlin article summarizes the concern this way: "For 350 years, men outnumbered women on college campuses. Now, in every state, every income bracket, every racial and ethnic group, and most industrialized Western nations, women reign, earning an average 57 percent of all B.A.'s and 58 percent of all master's degrees in the U.S. alone. There are 133 girls getting B.A.'s for every 100 guys—a number that's projected to grow to 142 women per 100 men by 2010, according to the U.S. Education Dept. If current trends continue, demographers say, there will be 156 women per 100 men earning degrees by 2020" (p. 2).

Morehouse College, the largest men's college in the country, has been investigating this issue under the leadership of President Walter Massey. The first meeting of men's colleges in America was held at Morehouse as part of a symposium he envisioned, "Reconnecting Males to Liberal Arts Campuses" (Massey, 2001). He invited the presidents of Wabash College, Hampden-Sydney College, and Saint John's University to join with Morehouse and a distinguished set of educators in analyzing this topic and working together to establish some next steps. Massey's vision was to focus on what he saw as more than an enrollment crisis for African American men—what looked like a crisis for all college men. Among the key findings of the conference was the conclusion that there is indeed a problem with enrollment, retention, and academic performance of college men, but it is most acute among at-risk men (African American, Native American, Latino, and low-income white males), and the situation is particularly acute at liberal arts colleges.

Recommendations for further research to guide policy development had implications for colleges and universities. Some of the key recommendations put forth were to focus on the successes already identified by all-male institutions, understand male learning styles, apply what we know to pedagogy, pursue a men's studies approach to the problem, form alliances with women's studies scholars, avoid changes that might help males at the expense of females, and encourage collaboration among institutions to result in better male outcomes.

The idea for this monograph was conceived at the symposium. This was my first visit to Morehouse; I went as the designated representative for Brother Dietrich Reinhart, president of Saint John's University, the second largest men's college, eager to meet colleagues from the other men's schools. We were asked to participate in a session exploring the hypothesis that there might be something that men's colleges have been doing to more successfully educate men that is worth investigating and understanding.

Creating a partnership between the two largest men's colleges seemed like a good place to start. I approached Obie Clayton, of the Morehouse Research Institute, and Eddie Gaffney, dean of student services, to write about the results of the symposium and to continue the conversation between our two men's institutions. Michael Kimmel's contribution to the symposium included a serious challenge to men's colleges to also educate their students in gender awareness. It seemed clear from Kimmel's comments that to understand college men we needed not only to understand what we were doing as men's colleges but also to accelerate our work on men's studies and involve scholars in the field of gender studies.

As there is only one men's studies minor in the country (at Hobart and William Smith Colleges), we thought naturally to call Rocco ("Chip") Capraro, associate dean, to get his perspective on these issues. As understanding men's studies necessitates understanding women's studies, we thought also of our colleagues at our partner women's institutions and accelerated our dialogues with Spelman College and the College of Saint Benedict. The relationship of our men's colleges to our sister women's colleges is analogous to that of men's studies and women's studies. If we were to try to better understand how men were faring in colleges, we would need to understand men in both single-sex and coeducational environments. Gender studies would help us do that. It might also assist us in consciously constructing learning environments for men on more than our all-male campuses.

We decided to look specifically at men's involvement in academic and student affairs programs and services; the patterns in a number of areas raised concern to a higher level.

According to a study of gender differences in the use of time for college first-year students from 1987 to 2002, not only was the percentage of males spending six or more hours per week in studying less than that of female college students at the end of the study (26.9 percent for males and 38.7

percent for females) but the declining time commitment for men was greater than that for women, 14.5 percent to 13.5 percent (Sax and others, 2002).

According to the Institute of International Education, during the academic year 2000–01 only about 35 percent of Americans students who studied in a foreign country and receiving academic credit from their home institution were male (Sharon Witherell, personal communication, March 2003).

Of the college students who participate in service, 35 percent of them are male, according to the Campus Compact Annual Service Statistics (Salgado, 2003). Of the college students who are involved in service, 10 percent are African American, 7 percent Asian American, 71 percent Caucasian, 7 percent Hispanic, 2 percent Native American, and 9 percent other. In 2002, the median hours of volunteering per week for first-year men was 0.6; for women it was 1.3. Of first-year women, 54.1 percent volunteered more than one hour per week, as opposed to 38.5 percent of first-year men. Between 1987 and 2002, volunteerism increased for both cohorts, though more sharply for women, such that the percentage of freshmen men doing more than one hour of volunteering per week rose by 12.2 percent; for women it rose 24.4 percent (Sax and others, 2002).

According to 1999–2000 U.S. Department of Education Postsecondary data, TRIO (Talent Search, Upward Bound, and Student Support Services) program participation rates have not been gender-balanced. Of the 328,070 participants in the Talent Search program, 40 percent were male. Of the 10,712 participants in the EOC (Educational Opportunity Centers) program, 36 percent were male. In the McNair graduate school preparation program, with 10,712 students participating, 34 percent were male.

Neil Murray, director of career services at the University of California-San Diego, recently reflected on serving men in college career centers: "We have mounds of evidence to document a simple but rarely stated fact— many of our services are extraordinarily underused by men. On several occasions I have raised the issue of gender disparity with groups of colleagues. Nearly everyone acknowledges this gap. . . . they report being surprised at the strength and consistency of the pattern but no one has reported trying to rectify it" (Murray, 2002, p. 26). The national career development organizations do not keep track of service use by gender, and few if any conference presentations exist on gender use of career services.

Perhaps nowhere is the situation more critical than in college men's health. Will Courtenay has written extensively on the topic that men do not engage in health prevention strategies or use health center services. With a higher suicide rate among college men and the fact that, overall, men are dying six to seven years younger than women, it is not an exaggeration to say that this topic is actually about saving men's lives (Courtenay, McCreary, and Merighi, 2002).

Even in voting, the pattern persists. Voter turnout among youths eighteen to twenty-four has declined steadily since 1972. Young women now turn out at 43 percent, and young men at 40 percent with the rate also declining faster for young men. This pattern persisted with white, black, and Hispanic men, but not Asians (Belsie, 2002).

The more we looked, the more we found data that indicated there was a bigger problem than male academic performance and persistence. We found what looked to be a pattern of disengagement or disconnection that might be growing. In fact, we found numerous examples of student affairs or academic affairs professional organizations not even keeping data by gender, and hence unaware of national patterns of how their programs were affecting men and women. If there were so few data and so few schools focusing on this aspect of education, then implementation of the Morehouse recommendations to focus not just on men but on the race, class, and gender dynamics of men's education would be even more difficult. This obviously needed more study.

It therefore seemed like a good idea to try to create a monograph to share what we were finding and identify some of the conversations and collaborations now developing that would, we hope, add to the national dialogue. We did not feel we had all the answers, but we certainly had enough questions. This writing has been an evolving process. You might liken it to the approach used by Spike Lee in his 1996 movie *Get on the Bus,* about the Million Man March. He filmed the journey of a fictitious bus load of marchers on their way to Washington. Each of the authors in this issue of *New Directions for Student Services* has a seat on our bus, as they share their work and participate in the discussions that occurred as the monograph took shape. Several author meetings were held with various groups of authors meeting at conferences, or at Morehouse or Saint John's, to talk about the project. What emerged is a dynamic conversation that is continuing. This issue is a progress report on how far we have come.

The first chapter, written by sociologists Obie Clayton and Cynthia Lucas Hewitt and Dean Eddie Gaffney from Morehouse, describes the symposium held there and the findings that came out of those meetings. Their focus is on male enrollment, retention, academic success, and engagement academically, the discussions held, and some of the reasons for lower male performance. They conclude by describing the symposia recommendations as well as a national agenda for action.

The first author meeting was held at Morehouse and involved scholars from Morehouse, Spelman College, and Hobart and William Smith Colleges. At that meeting one of our main issues began to appear. It was the same as what Michael Kimmel raised at the second symposium: How do we address the issues raised by the Morehouse symposia from a men's studies perspective? Chip Capraro introduces that topic in Chapter Two; he takes the process a step further and shows how to apply men's studies to particular student affairs programs and services such as alcohol education and sexual assault/harassment education to overcome the common problem of creating resistance in men who are the subjects of these sessions.

In the third chapter, Cynthia Spence, from Spelman College, speaks about her experience and that of Spelman working with Morehouse, and how their colleges have collaborated to design educational environments for "the Morehouse Man and the Spelman Woman." She makes a compelling case that women's colleges, though empowering women to take leadership positions in society, have also intentionally educated women in gender awareness. Her challenge to Morehouse—and, I would add, to other colleges educating men—is to educate men not simply for leadership roles but also in gender roles by such activities as creating a safe place for men to express their emotions and understand society's messages on masculinity. Manju Parikh, from the College of Saint Benedict, shares how she has taken up this task by integrating the education of men from a men's studies perspective and the education of women from the perspective of women's studies in the classroom.

How the College of Saint Benedict and Saint John's University are intentionally designing their learning environments for men and women could also be of interest to coeducational institutions. These colleges, sponsored by Benedictine monasteries and historically founded for women and men, possess wisdom about how to intentionally design individual and collective men's and women's learning environments.

Tracy Davis and Jason Laker together have served in the capacity of chair of the American College Personnel Associations's (ACPA) Standing Committee for Men for the past eight years; in addition to knowing a great deal about this topic and teaching it in both undergraduate and student affairs graduate settings, they have become familiar with many of the people and programs attempting to address these issues. Their chapter includes some examples of successful programs and services for men at other colleges.

The fifth chapter presents a framework for designing effective programs and services consistent with men's theory; it also describes some of the barriers to this work. One serious matter discussed is the lack of preparation for student affairs professionals in their preprofessional programs. Echoing a theme from other chapters, the authors argue that effective programs must challenge and support college men as well as draw upon theoretical and practical understanding of men's identity development. They expand this theory to include the multiple dimensions of identity development: sexual orientation, race, culture, class, and gender.

The first time I realized there was a serious problem with men in higher education was in reading the work of Will Courtenay. His extensive research and careful articulation of how men are dying seven years younger than women and how the trend is reflected on college campuses, most seriously in suicide statistics, was a wake-up call for me. His chapter should convince the reader that this is not just a matter of reducing attrition and increasing enrollment for men in college; it also saves men's lives.

The sixth chapter, by Randall Ludeman of Bemidji State University, addresses an area of campus life where men are more engaged than women:

campus judicial systems. Arguing that we need to better understand the links between socially constructed masculinity and violence, he focuses on the critical element of men's emotional development. By drawing on men's studies, student affairs administrators responsible for student discipline can better understand the cases they adjudicate with men and transform these systems so as to empower these students to learn a broader range of emotional expressiveness.

In the concluding chapter, Merle Longwood and Mark Muesse, co-editors of *Redeeming Men: Religion and Masculinities* (Boyd, Longwood, and Muesse, 1996), write (with William Schipper) about college men's spirituality. At a time when traditional masculinity makes it difficult for men to acknowledge their spiritual nature, the latest Higher Education Research Institute (HERI) study shows a keen interest in spirituality from the majority of college students in their survey of twenty-five thousand (Young, 2003). This chapter presents a successful program that meets the need for men to connect to themselves and to other men on an intimate level. This process for creating safe spaces, referred to in several of the preceding chapters, and a process of creating adult mentors are described and adapted for replication on other campuses. The issue ends, therefore, on a hopeful note that focusing on men's holistic development—most notably, spiritual development—helps men connect more fully with other men and with themselves. Our last author meeting was held at a February 2004 conference on the college male, with Jackson Katz, Don McPherson, Harry Brod, and more than 170 registrants. One key theme from the conference was the need for making men whole (or the making of whole men). It therefore seems like a fitting conclusion for this issue.

Michael Kimmel writes the Afterword, which pulls the chapters together in a focus on engaging men as men in the richness and variations of their lives. He reminds us our journey has just begun and challenges us to a more complete look at college men and masculinities including gay men. That work is already under way in preparation for future publications from the men's center.

There are many others to acknowledge for their work on this issue. Brother Aaron Raverty, O.S.B., from Saint John's Liturgical Press, has lent invaluable expertise; Harry Brod, his sage advice; JoAnn Carlson, her technical skill; my family (Kolleen, Meg, Gus, Toc), their support; Malcolm Williams, his wisdom; and research assistance came from Gavin Poindexter, Steve Dehmer, Mike Brakke, Marc Hedman-Dennis, Danjel Lozancic, Amy Barsness, and Adam Beatty.

Gar E. Kellom
Editor

References

Belsie, L. "Men Lag Women in the Voting Booth." *Christian Science Monitor,* Feb. 28, 2002, p. 4.

Boyd, S. B., Longwood, W. M., and Muesse, M. W. (eds.). *Redeeming Men: Religion and Masculinities.* Louisville, Ky.: Westminster/John Knox Press, 1996.

Conlin, M. "The New Gender Gap: From Kindergarten to Grad School, Boys Are Becoming the Second Sex." *Business Week Online,* May 26, 2003, p. 2.

Courtenay, W. H., McCreary, D. R., and Merighi, J. R. "Gender and Ethnic Differences in Health Beliefs and Behaviors." *Journal of Health Psychology,* 2002, 7(3), 219–231.

Hacker, A. "How the B.A. Gap Widens the Chasm Between Men and Women." *Chronicle of Higher Education,* June 30, 2003, p. B10.

Kellom, G. "Improving the Recruitment, Education, and Retention of Men in Residential Colleges and Universities." Paper presented at the Oxford Roundtable on Residential Colleges, Pembroke College, July 1999.

Massey, W. E. "Men on Our Campuses: A Summary Report from Reconnecting Males to Liberal Education, A Morehouse College Symposium on Higher Education's Shifting Gender Balance." Report of symposium distributed to participants, Apr. 2–4, 2001, Atlanta.

Murray, N. "Engaging Male Students in Career Planning: How Practitioners Can Bridge the Gender Gap." *NACE Journal,* Winter 2002, pp. 25–27.

Salgado, D. M. "2003 Campus Compact Annual Membership Survey." http://www.compact.org/newscc/stats 2003. Accessed June 16, 2004.

Sax, L. J., and others. "The American Freshman: National Norms for Fall 2002." Los Angeles: Higher Education Research Institute, UCLA, 2002.

U.S. Department of Education, Office of PostSecondary Education. "Federal TRIO Programs." Retrieved Aug. 13, 2003, from http://www.ed.gov/about/offices/list/ope/trio/index.html.

Young, J. "Most Students Care Strongly About Religion or Spirituality, Survey Finds." *Chronicle of Higher Education,* Nov. 28, 2003. http://chronicle.com/prm/daily/2003/11/2003112102.htm. Accessed Dec. 1, 2003.

GAR E. KELLOM *received his Ph.D. from the Graduate Theological Union and the University of California, Berkeley, in history and phenomenology of religion and has served as a chief student affairs officer for twenty years, and as director of the Saint John's men's center since 2002.*

1

This chapter summarizes the recommendations from a Morehouse College symposium on higher education's shifting gender balance, Men on Our Campuses: Reconnecting Males to Liberal Education.

Reflecting on Reconnecting Males to Higher Education

Obie Clayton, Cynthia Lucas Hewitt, Eddie D. Gaffney

What are the causes of the deepening crisis of disconnect between young black men and educational institutions, particularly higher education institutions, and what can be done about it? Recently, this question was posed in relation to the experience of young men in general, whose postsecondary enrollment, across the board, is becoming disparately low in comparison with women. In April 2001, Morehouse College convened a two-day symposium entitled Reconnecting Males to Liberal Education; it attracted a diverse group of nearly one hundred scholars, policy makers, community leaders, and students from around the country to begin planning a long-term effort to address the declining fortunes of males in higher education. Increasingly, there is questioning as to whether educational disparities are a problem of young black and other minority men, or of all young men across race—particularly those of lower socioeconomic status. The conference focused on establishing the degree to which a trend of low and declining completion of a college education is occurring and affecting males—African American, Native American, Hispanic, and indeed all male youths—and how ongoing discriminatory practices in education contribute to this outcome.

This chapter summarizes the conference findings on factors contributing to the often low achievement outcomes of males, and black males in particular, at the K–12 as well as postsecondary education levels; presents a review of what is known theoretically about the causes; and discusses the question of building a research agenda. The goal is to raise questions to stimulate research that is not focused simply on observing trends but rather

NEW DIRECTIONS FOR STUDENT SERVICES, no. 107, Fall 2004 © Wiley Periodicals, Inc.

on understanding successful education initiatives, and assessing the extent of their generalizability, as a foundation for policy enactment.

This study took as its starting premise the importance of a college degree to earning power, and this earning power to stability of families, both nuclear and extended. A low number of black men prepared for jobs requiring a college degree and providing better-than-average earnings impedes family formation, pushes up household poverty rates, and contributes to the likelihood of social disorder. A college education is also critical in developing the abstract thinking necessary to comprehend the processes that affect our lives in a globalized economy, and to participate effectively in the political arena and civil society. The increasing relative success of women in academics may become both the effect and an effective cause of structural shifts in social organizations, including schools, workplaces, and cultural arenas, that provide hospitable and embracing environments for women but may affect male development negatively. Our findings suggest that the relevance of a college degree, and a liberal arts degree in particular, should not be taken for granted; instead, it may be a starting point for investigating this trend of disengagement.

The Situation

As reported at the conference, in 1995–96 approximately 37 percent of the black undergraduate student population under age twenty-five were men, and the disparity among older undergrads was even larger, as we encounter the phenomenon that people who return to enroll in college at an older age are disproportionately female. Only Native Americans suffer a larger gender gap in college enrollment, with young men making up only 30 percent of enrolled students (King, 2000). In 1999, black men earned 36 percent of the bachelor's degrees awarded to African Americans (U.S. Census, 2000). In general, the gender gap is concentrated among low-income students. Among all low-income students, males constitute 44 percent; among low-income whites, they are 46 percent; for African Americans, they are 32 percent; for Native Americans, 23 percent, and for those of Hispanic ethnicity, 43 percent. Only among Asian Americans do males retain a majority, 53 percent. In midrange and higher-income households in general, young men tend to be equally represented, 50 percent and 51 percent, respectively. Among blacks, however, there remains a substantial gender gap even at higher income levels, as men make up 41 percent of the upper-income black students (King, 2000).

Beyond male-female gaps, the prevalence of a college education among black men is significantly low. In Georgia, the recent task force on black male education of the Board of Regents found that fewer than 2 percent of the students at the state's main research institution, the University of Georgia, were black men, in a state where they number roughly 17 percent of public school enrollment. The ratio of black women to black men there is two to one, a rate typical for Georgia's public college campuses (McCarthy, 2002).

The question is whether, in general, men are a declining portion of students enrolled in higher education. At the conference, it was reported (based on National Center for Education Statistics data) that in 1998 men were 43 percent of students, down from 48 percent in 1985, and their representation is expected to continue to decline to 42 percent of students enrolled by 2010 ("Men on Our Campuses," 2001). However, even though 2000 data show this ratio holding, 2001 data show a reversal, as men make up 48.6 percent of the population enrolled in college (U.S. Department of Labor, 2002). Are these fluctuations or are they trends—and even if fluctuations, are there gendered patterns? There are other figures that raise concern. In terms of bachelor's degrees conferred, men amount to only 43 percent of the recipients in 2000–01. The higher male proportion of the enrolled student population in 2001 should result in a greater gender parity of degrees earned in two or three years, unless gender differences in retention, or in enrollment by type of college, come into play. Beginning in 1980, attainment at the master's level by women has also increasingly come to surpass that of men (U.S. Department of Education, 2002).

It is in the area of liberal arts education that disparities are particularly apparent. Even where overall underrepresentation is not occurring, men are underrepresented in particular fields, notably education, psychology, communications, and public administration, and in the institutions focusing on those areas (liberal arts colleges). For instance, Dickinson College reports that in 1999, before their innovative recruitment efforts reversed the decline, only 36 percent of the freshman class was male ("Men on Our Campuses," 2001).

The significance of this lower representation of men in general among college enrollment remained a question on which assessments differed. Many concluded that when the gap is examined, it is apparent that the majority of male students are doing fine; it is among men of color and white men at the lower end of the socioeconomic scale that substantial problems exist. Others, particularly those focused on liberal arts education, see fundamental problems in connection with male students. Jacqueline King, of the American Council on Education, cautions that much of the gender gap can be attributed to the major influx of older women into college in the 1980s and 1990s (King, 2000). However, even when data are reported for only age twenty-four and younger, disparities are still seen.

Circumstances That Result in Underrepresentation

The low representation of black men obtaining a college degree, in particular, is fueled by disparities in the number of black male youths who graduate from high school, take college preparatory courses, score adequately on achievement tests, and have the financial wherewithal to attend college. Of those black male youths who do enroll in college, many fall victim to problems that make achieving an acceptable level of retention a critical factor. In general, circumstances that result in underrepresentation of black male students in college begin long before freshman year. Overwhelmingly, the K–12 school system is failing to impart to black male youths the skills and aspirations necessary to enter, persist, and obtain a higher education degree.

Theoretical Approaches to Understanding

Black men's struggles for success in education can be better understood by looking at factors such as cultural resistance, gender identity, availability of black teachers, and societal priorities.

Institutional Racism and Cultural Resistance. Approaches to understanding the root causes of this disparity in successful college graduation for males, and black males in particular, have tended to fall into the category of those focusing on how schools are failing children—structural explanations—and those pointing to cultural differences as the source of the problem. Structural analyses have identified provision of unequal amounts of information (the failure of schools to offer equal instruction, adequate curricula, and challenging and developmental assignments) particularly through tracking, as the central reason for unequal outcomes by race. Such unequal access in a public institution—the school—is essentially a gross violation of the student's constitutional right to an equal education in all respects. This is one of the most significant types of institutional racism forming the bedrock of the continuing significance of racism and discrimination.

Although the continuing failure of American society to provide equal education affects both black male and female youths, there is an added dimension of deprivation associated with male gender, given the social hierarchy. Overall, it has been found that discrimination takes the form of attempts to exclude blacks from leadership and social control roles, which white males are groomed to fill. The overwhelmingly superior academic performance among many groups of Asian heritage—shown in their increasingly disproportionate presence in colleges—should translate into a disproportionate presence in boardrooms and political leadership positions across America, but this has not occurred. In fact, it was only with the universalistic gains resulting from the civil rights struggles that citizens of Asian heritage began to see such positions open up to them (Jiobu, 1988; Onishi, 1996; U.S. Commission on Civil Rights, 1988).

Black male youths, by virtue of being male, are imbued with an expectation of high status, yet by virtue of being African or minority they are identified within the American social stratification system with low status; hence low expectations are conveyed by the dominant ideological state structure—the schools. Many black and low-income youths appear to "penetrate" the achievement ideology and recognize that they are not well placed to obtain one of the limited number of privileged slots available. This realization is reflected in the lack of teacher expectancy, support, and encouragement for black males in particular, and the prevalence of encountering school personnel who do not seem to care (Polite, 1999; Tucker and others, 2000). Then, understanding that they are not among essentially the top 20 percent or so, rather than competing they make the logical and common choice of electing not to try, not to engage, as argued by Arthur Combs in *Myths in Education* (1979). This status inconsistency may be resolved in the only way that offers the youths some control over the criteria: rejection of identification with the American achievement ideology and commitment to an alternative community criterion for success.

Given the range of identity options people are exposed to, they elect to fashion their self-identity around goals that are attainable, and hence supportive of a sense of personal efficacy. Thus at the root of what may be viewed as an "aberrant" black male youth culture is adoption of an identity structure independent of the "American identity" connected to the universalistic achievement ethos. Black male youth subcultures may be fashioned around an alternative, possibly oppositional, identity structure that includes limited academic criteria. Osborne's studies (1999) of African American boys' identification with academics showed a dramatic decrease between the eighth and tenth grades, with further decrease by grade twelve. Further, this disidentification has increased over time, from 1972, when appreciable racial differences were not apparent, to 1992, when such differences were significant and substantial.

Gender Identity and Attitudes Toward Academics: Are Male Roles Changing? There is also considerable evidence of not only status inconsistency for youth who are male and black but also compounding effects of what we may term male "role strain." The male role set traditionally valorized in American society for white males was characterized by competitive, relatively aggressive behavior; lack of competition by females; freedom from repetitive, detailed tasks that require tact and discipline; and expectation of preeminence, or privilege. Attitudes boys and girls have toward specific academic subjects and how they relate to their own gender identities appear to influence their performance in different subjects. Math and science are more often associated with masculinity, while humanities and the social sciences can require skills and attributes more often associated with feminine behavior. This is not categorical. Clearly the humanities and social sciences were locations where the national identity was defined through the telling of history, enshrinement of a philosophical base, propagation of forms of nationalism, and legitimation of the stratification system. This was done primarily by men and serves one of the major realms of social power. However, shifts in the locus of these "latent pattern maintenance functions," to use the concept of Talcott Parsons (1977), may be at the heart of a shift in male choices among disciplines, as economists replace philosophers and engineers replace social scientists. Unraveling these complex trends in social stratification may help explain the relatively smaller male pool for liberal arts.

Thus it is an open question whether and to what extent male roles are changing, whether they are retaining essential characteristics, and whether they should take on new characteristics to adapt to changing social structures. Kimmel presented the suggestion that masculinity is too narrowly defined in our culture. Consequently, males shun behavior outside of the type described here and react to the evolving social conditions that are inviting their interest with rejection, instead adopting hypermasculinity to compensate. This is consonant with the work of Paul Willis (1977). He finds in his classic study of low-income (working-class) youth in England that the patriarchal element of their male culture ensured that they remained focused on manual pursuits; thus—despite their apprehension that they would lack opportunity in their place in the social structure—they did not seek to change their male role conception by developing skills perceived as unmasculine that would offer them white-collar jobs. Brenda Bankart, a psychologist attending the conference, also suggested that society gives boys too narrow a portal through which to express themselves as males.

One of the outcomes of the conference was endorsement of the need to study and know what constitutes male traits—perhaps by way of masculinity studies. Because of their hegemony historically, men have not been spurred to carry out the self-conscious evaluation "minorities" have undertaken, which resulted in the conscious attempt to shape structures to adjust for and accommodate to factors unique to the group that are a locus of disadvantage. Studies have documented evidence to show that boys tend to thrive in educational environments that are competitive and include at least some degree of physical activity ("Men on Our Campuses," 2001). However, it is not clear whether school districts have incorporated this information into their pedagogy; given the trend toward added hours of core instruction—less time allotted for recess and recreation, or manual arts such as music and band—it seems unlikely that this has been done. (Interestingly, amid the explosion of attention to gender roles incited by the push for state recognition of gay marriages, there is sudden attention to the possible injustice and deleterious effects of having no recess time in Georgia schools—perhaps one arena of the structure of the school day particularly important to male youths.)

The Need for Cultural Congruence: The Struggle for Male and Minority Teachers. There is considerable evidence that the low number of minority, and black male, teachers in particular is a great hindrance to young black men successfully navigating the academic experience and emerging with the prerequisites for successful college completion. Black male educators and male single-sex schools may provide an optimal environment for success in increasing the pool of well-prepared black male college entrants. First, retention in high school is greatly affected by disciplinary actions.

Behaviors disproportionately identified with male culture are often the basis for disciplinary action, and far too often they become cause for suspension and expulsion, with the increased likelihood of termination of these youths' educational careers (Irvine, 1991). Again, being male and black compounds the difficulties (Blumenson and Nilsen, 2002). One known ameliorative factor is the presence of male teachers, particularly of the same race or ethnicity. There is a significant literature showing that teachers are less likely to deem inappropriate behavior sufficiently offensive to warrant bureaucratic disciplinary response, and more likely to attempt to cope with the behavior and change it, if it is understandable from within their social experiential base. Research has shown that men tend to be less affected by the spontaneous active and challenging behavior frequently encountered among boys, and they are more likely to praise and encourage them (Foster and Peele, 1999). In fact, successful African American teachers often develop a teaching style that capitalizes upon this type of outlook and expression (Slaughter-Defoe and Nakagawa, 1990; Lancer, 2002; Watson and Smitherman, 1996).

The statistics on black teachers, minority teachers, and black male teachers in particular are distinctly alarming, as was stressed at the conference ("Men on Our Campuses," 2001). African Americans in the teaching profession have declined from 8.6 percent of the teaching force in 1980 to 6.8 percent in 1994 (U.S. Department of Education, 1997). Central to the sharp decline in black teachers was the desegregation process (Meier, Stewart, and England, 1989). In terms of immediate causes, a National Education Association study concludes that "state-mandated testing policies and practices far outweigh all other often cited reasons for the minority teacher shortage," being responsible for elimination of an estimated 37,717 minority candidates for education schools and teachers, including 21,515 blacks (Smith, 1988, 1989). Clearly this finding relevant to black males is also of critical importance to all boys, particularly those of low socioeconomic status: Has there been a precipitous decline of male teachers, particularly in middle school and high school?

There is a need to increase recruitment, financial support for, and retention of black teachers. The work of Meier, Stewart, and England (1989) showed that this goal is furthered where there is a significant number of blacks in the higher administration of the educational system, and that the number of school administrators correlates directly with the level of black political representation at the local and regional levels. Key appointments and goal expectations are often set by the legislature and executive structure, and this translates into more hiring of minority administrators, who then select, support, and train as necessary more black school teachers. Again, the presence or absence of whites from lower-class backgrounds, traditionally supplied by the immigrant population, may also correlate with the presence or absence of their group in school administration, and ultimately among political representatives. In general, the discrepancy between black—and in particular, black male—outcomes and expected educational attainment is viewed by many as a political issue—essentially one of civil rights.

Economic Competition from the Work World, and the Cost of Education. Perhaps the most understudied question of critical impact is the effect on college aspirations of the assessment of the benefits of a college degree by recent graduates—the elder brothers, cousins, and friends of the young men as they are making their choice. Their experiences are a critical influence. On the basis of what is currently only anecdotal evidence, when asked young adults complain about the difficulty of obtaining a job commensurate with having a college degree, in the field in which she or he studied, and paying a decent wage. We have taken for granted the connect between education and job availability. Essentially, we may fall into the trap of misconstruing a rapid percentage rise among white-collar, skilled, and high-tech jobs for a major increase in the absolute number of jobs becoming available (Rothstein, 1999).

Saskia Sassen (1991) questioned viewing the shift to a service economy as exemplary of upward mobility to white-collar work. She points to the need for a disproportionate number of low-skilled workers where the number of high-skilled workers is expanding, because *the latter employ the former* for multiple tasks, such as child care, food prep, home and clothing cleaning, and so on. Further, as even Robert Reich (1992), secretary of labor in the Clinton administration, points out, only the nonroutinized jobs—the "symbolic analyst" jobs involving cutting-edge problem defining and solving through networking and resource mobilization—are likely to continue to be high-paid. This distinction is not based on the college major, degree, or occupation, but on the nature of the job, whether it is connected to a knowledge-intensive, cutting-edge production setting, or whether it involves repetitive tasks. In general, we may be guilty of underestimating the salience and impact of the folk knowledge that young men are operating under when they make decisions about college, as popularized in the bestseller *Rich Dad, Poor Dad.* Understanding the apprehension of this situation on the part of young men, how they make sense of this, and why it may lead to gender-specific outcomes is critical to connecting males to postsecondary education.

On the other side of the equation, at the high school level competing forces tend to lure young men away from school and into the workforce early. Increasingly, the unrelenting consumerist orientation is leading to a culture where purchases mediate identity formation (Lasn, 2000). Who you are is what you buy, display, and consume. Identities, from the generic to the more discrete and unique, are available for sale.

The pull on young men may be more intensive. The forces for consumerism have in relatively recent years successfully revolutionized the role of the male from primarily earner to consumer, and among youth we may find that by gender he is the larger consumer. The successful linking of icons of male-centered culture (sports and sport figures in particular) to items marketed for identity (sport shoes, jerseys, and so on) is a major innovation (Gereffi, 1993; Mies, 2001). Further, car culture and technology culture (cell phones, computer games, and so on) have also greatly extended the commercialization of what have been historically masculine traits. In particular, Thomas Mortenson pointed out that male earning power is greater than that of females immediately after high school and thus may exert a disproportionate pull into the labor force for them. In 1997 men earned $22,440 compared to $15,789 for women, a pattern that held for all races ("Men on Our Campuses," 2001). On the other hand, the cost of higher education has continued to escalate, perhaps forcing the issue of long-term debt and circumscribed discretionary income. These trends may reinforce the pressure on youths to become consumers, and to take jobs before finishing school—leading perhaps to not graduating, or graduating but not going to college.

There is also a general trend of decreasing real purchasing power, such that the one-earner middle-class family has increasingly given way to the two-earner family, which in its turn now is being supplanted by the multiple-earner family model (Schor, 1992). For African Americans, who in the aggregate have approximately 11 percent of the wealth of white American families, there is often little or no savings to be invested in providing identity consumption to their children so they can have the leisure to focus on their studies (Oliver and Shapiro, 1995). Further, money-seeking activities may not only compete successfully with their academic commitments but even destroy their academic future if they include illegal activities. Clearly, these same forces are likely to be at work among low-income families.

Incarceration and Criminalization. Finally, in the quest for resources and status, too many young black men become involved with criminal activities, which can lead to criminal careers if incarceration is the social sanction applied. Increasingly, issues and situations that were handled on a case-by-case basis within schools and with the parents are now required to be submitted as part of the de jure legal record, with prescribed negative effects on a student's ability to remain in school or receive financial aid for college. Blumenson and Nilsen (2002) point out that the war on drugs, combined with the zero-tolerance policies enacted by those states containing 88 percent of public schools, led to the suspension of 3.1 million students and expulsion of 87,000 in the 1998 school year. Mandatory punishments are applied in a draconian way without distinction between true threats of violence and genuinely low-risk situations. Impelled by the spate of in-school violence in the 1990s, legislators reacted by casting "all students as objects of worry and suspicion" and establishing systems of surveillance (Blumenson and Nilsen, 2002, p. 5).

According to one study cited, approximately 80 percent of students charged with drug or alcohol infractions are suspended or expelled from school, no matter how insignificant the amount. African American students are expelled from school at twice the rate of white students, and although

African Americans are 13 percent of all monthly drug users they are 55 percent of those convicted of drug possession and 74 percent of those sentenced to prison for possession (Blumenson and Nilsen, 2002). Students convicted of a drug offense have been made either temporarily or permanently ineligible for federal college loans and grants by the Drug Free Student Loans Act of 1998. For those in prison, access to Pell Grants was terminated by law in 1994. Blumenson and Nilsen write: "The war on drugs has spawned a second front—a war on education. The casualties of this war are all poor or lower-income people who cannot afford to buy a private education" (Blumenson and Nilsen, 2002, p. 4).

Factors of Success: Directions for Future Research

There is an emerging body of research on single-sex education that overwhelmingly reports positive effects for boys when attending all-male schools. Historically, the issue of single-sex education has been posed in terms of creating conditions where the needs of female students could be addressed. Now this understanding of the gender specificity of developmental patterns is being employed to explain beneficial effects found in all-male schooling environments (National Association for Single-Sex Education, 2002; Riordan, 2003). Single-sex schools have reported major declines in disciplinary problems and test score improvement, and gains in academic achievement and educational aspirations, improved self-control by students, decreased sex role stereotyping, and better attitudes and behaviors related to academics. Single-sex school graduates are more likely to have considered graduate school, and those of both genders attended colleges that were more selective than their coed counterparts (Lee and Bryk, 1986; Lee and Marks, 1990). Watson and Smitherman (1996), in their assessment of the Malcolm X Academy in Detroit, place emphasis on the all-male nature of the school and the educational perspective these innovators also brought to the effort: "an African-centered educational philosophy and program can influence the attitudes, behavior, and educational performance of Black male students. . . . grounded in the human need for identity, purpose, and knowledge of self" (p. 94). Another significant factor they point to is their "acceptance of the fact that boys and girls learn and develop differently" (p. 95). Further research is required to answer the question of whether self-selection by parents, students, and teachers of single-sex schools reflects a prior existing difference in value orientation in comparison with those who select coeducational schools; hence, generalizing the model may not generalize the results. Results may stem from the greater cultural coherence between same-sex participants, or simply from involvement with an experimental project.

Until today, these experiments with single-sex education in public schools had to be organized under some other stated principle because of

Title IX of the Civil Rights Act of 1972, intended to prohibit sexual discrimination; however, legislation is expected to pass that frees educators to develop single-sex schooling (Raspberry, 2002).

Research-Guided Policy Development

What follows are the areas identified at the Morehouse Conference for further research as a foundation for policy development.

- Longitudinal studies, particularly of tracking and the placement of minority and lower-class males, should be carried out, including looking at the role of counselors, teachers, parents, and the student, seeking to highlight "hotspots" across the sixteen-year continuum.
- Research efforts should focus on successes: though many young black men are struggling in school, some have achieved marked success. In this regard, there is a need to look closely at the successes of all-male education, particularly in light of the anticipated regulatory changes to Title IX that would permit same-gender education in publicly funded institutions.
- Study of the social structural barriers, particularly racism, shaping the learning environment experienced by black male students is important. Investigation should also focus on the degree and ways in which environmental and cultural forces influence minority males' perceptions, and valuation, of education. The key here is the study of consumerism and its differential effects on young men and young women. It is also important to investigate the structure of the labor market and the response of young men to it, particularly how college graduates are assessing the situation to their peers.
- There is a need to better understand male learning styles and interaction. At each level, do males have special learning needs? If so, how can they be met? Can we learn anything from the previous focus on women? We need to know whether information on boys' learning styles is filtering into school pedagogy, and with what results? What is the impact of the gender of a child's teacher on the student's overall academic performance, and what can be done to increase the prevalence of male teachers, particularly of racial-minority and low-income background?
- To understand the trends occurring, it is important to look carefully at disaggregated data and analyze the interaction of gender, race, and class for students and teachers. More detailed research on African American, Native American, and Latino males, among whom a large number of at-risk males are found, would provide a base of comparative information. There is also a need for information that considers class or socioeconomic status, along with race and gender, since across race lower-class males show various degrees of disadvantage. Analysis of disaggregated disciplinary data is important to understand the trajectory that leads to failure to complete high school.

• Attention should be focused on assessing what we know about best practices for retention of male students in college and high school, a critical need. In this regard, Morehouse College has a particular commitment to address black male educational performance and retention issues and should take leadership in this area.

Policy Implications

The actions listed here are recommended specifically for higher education institutions seeking to address the issues surrounding at-risk men.

• Increase efforts at retention.
• Pursue modification in recruitment, such as that pioneered by Dickinson in 1999 (when only 36 percent of the freshman class was male); maybe appeal to the career focus of many male students.
• Encourage collaboration between colleges and universities in fulfilling these tasks.
• Provide incentives for colleges and universities to place restoring and maintaining gender balance high on their list of priorities.
• Strive to increase the number of minority males in the administrative and professional ranks of higher education, and of K–12.
• Develop stronger partnerships with educators at the K–12 level as well as with business and community service, and focus parental attention on these issues.
• Create incentives to educators to produce better outcomes for male students at every level.
• Aim to position this issue as an alliance with feminism; policies that might help male students at the expense of females should be avoided.

Conclusion: National Action Agenda

Making an impact on the problem of black men, and all men, who are at risk for disengagement from academics and a low rate of college attendance and completion requires a concerted effort between research and community action. Although we seek to understand the causes, we must also seek to understand the array of forces, particularly those positive to change, that have not been strengthened to overcome the forces of inertia and decline. It is important that our research efforts tie into better strategies to convey information about male academic performance to families so they can keep their sons from sliding away from the college-bound pipeline.

Second, it is critical that we hold accreditation agencies accountable for selecting a pool of educational professionals representative of the communities they must serve. It is not enough to have abstract standards if they serve to create an alienating environment without cultural congruence for black youths, males in particular. This is not an equal education. We must also collaborate effectively with after-school providers, such as faith communities and businesses, as partners, particularly given the difficulty some parents experience in furnishing academic support for their children. Given the large number of young men behind bars, particularly those of low socioeconomic background, and African American and minority males in particular, greater availability of education in prisons should be pursued. Finally, we look forward to the development of a statement of principles to be adopted by the Morehouse-led group, to focus attention on principles and models of successful male education, and to garner public attention.

References

Blumenson, E., and Nilsen, E. S. "How to Create an Underclass, or How the War on Drugs Became a War on Education." (Working Paper 1.) *Suffolk University Law School Faculty Publications,* Dec. 2002. *http://www.law.suffolk.edu/faculty/eblumens/underclassarticlegalleys.pdf.* Retrieved June 30, 2004.

Combs, A. *Myths in Education.* Boston: Allyn and Bacon, 1979.

Foster, M., and Peele, T. "Teaching Black Males: Lessons from the Experts." In V. Polite (ed.), *African American Males in School and Society.* New York: Teachers College Press, 1999.

Gereffi, G. "The Organization of Buyer-Driven Global Commodity Chains: How U.S. Retailers Shape Overseas Production Networks." In G. Gereffi and M. Korzeiniewicz (eds.), *Commodity Chains and Global Capitalism.* Westport, Conn.: Greenwood Press, 1993.

Irvine, J. *Black Students and School Failure.* New York: Praeger, 1991.

Jiobu, R. M. "Ethnic Hegemony and the Japanese of California." *American Sociological Review,* 1988, *53,* 353–367.

King, J. E. "Gender Equity in Higher Education: Are Male Students at a Disadvantage?" Washington, D.C.: American Council of Education, Center for Policy Analysis, 2000.

Lancer, J. "Courting Success: A New Method for Motivating Urban Black Males." *Black Issues in Higher Education,* 2002, *19*(3), 34.

Lasn, K. *Culture Jam.* New York: HarperCollins, 2000.

Lee, V. E., and Bryk, A. S. "Effects of Single-Sex Secondary Schools on Students' Achievement and Attitudes." *Journal of Educational Psychology,* 1986, *78*(5), 381–395.

Lee, V. E., and Marks, H. "Sustained Effects of the Single-Sex Secondary School Experience on Attitudes, Behaviors, and Values in College." *Journal of Educational Psychology,* 1990, *82,* 578–592.

McCarthy, R. "Colleges Seek Black Men: Regents Study Targets Obstacles That Deter Enrollment in Georgia Universities." *Atlanta Journal Constitution,* Dec. 6, 2002, p. A1.

Meier, K. J., Stewart, J., Jr., and England, R. E. *Race, Class, and Education.* Madison: University of Wisconsin, 1989.

"Men on Our Campuses: A Summary Report from 'Reconnecting Males to Liberal Education,' a Morehouse College Symposium." April 2001, Atlanta.

Mies, M. *Patriarchy and Accumulation on a World Scale.* New York: Zed, 2001.

National Association for Single-Sex Education. "What's the Evidence? What Have Researchers Found When They Compare Single-Sex Education with Coeducation?" 2002. http://www.singlesexschools.org/evidence.html. Accessed April 10, 2004.

Oliver, M. L., and Shapiro, T. M. *Black Wealth/White Wealth.* New York: Routledge, 1995.

Onishi, N. "Affirmative Action: Choosing Sides." *New York Times,* Mar. 31, 1996 (Education Life), pp. 26–35.

Osborne, J. W. "Unraveling Underachievement Among African American Boys from an Identification with Academics Perspective." *Journal of Negro Education,* 1999, 68(4), 555–565.

Parsons, T. *Social Systems and the Evolution of Action Theory.* New York: Free Press, 1977.

Polite, V. C. *African American Males in School and Society.* New York: Teachers College Press, 1999.

Raspberry, W. "A Welcome Step Toward Single-Sex Classrooms." *Times Union* [Albany, N.Y.], May 13, 2002, p. A7.

Reich, R. *The Work of Nations.* New York: Vintage, 1992.

Riordan, C. *Equality and Achievement: An Introduction to the Sociology of Education.* Upper Saddle River, N.J.: Prentice Hall, 2003.

Rothstein, R. "Calculus for Waitresses? A 'New Economy' Myth." *New York Times,* Oct. 27, 1999, p. A12.

Sassen, S. *The Global City.* Princeton, N.J.: Princeton University Press, 1991.

Schor, J. B. *The Overworked American.* New York: Basic Books, 1992.

Slaughter-Defoe, D., and Nakagawa, K. "Toward Cultural/Ecological Perspectives on Schooling and Achievement in African- and Asian-American Children." *Child Development,* 1990, 61, 363–383.

Smith, G. "Tomorrow's White Teachers: A Response to the Holmes Group." *Journal of Negro Education,* 1988, 57(2), 178–194.

Smith, G. "The Effects of Competency Testing on the Supply of Minority Teachers." Report prepared for the National Education Association and the Council of Chief State School Officers. Washington, D.C., 1989. (ED 302 521)

Tucker, C. M., and others. "Student-Generated Solutions to Enhance the Academic Success of African American Youth." *Child Study Journal,* 2000, 30(3), 205–222.

U.S. Census Bureau. *Statistical Abstract of the United States: 2000.* Washington, D.C.: U.S. Census Bureau, 2000.

U.S. Commission on Civil Rights. "The Economic Status of Americans of Asian Descent: An Exploratory Investigation." Clearinghouse Publication 95. Washington, D.C.: U.S. Commission on Civil Rights, 1988.

U.S. Department of Education. "Schools and Staffing Survey, 1993–94," Washington, D.C.: National Center for Education Statistics, 1997.

U.S. Department of Labor. "College Enrollment and Work Activity of 2001 High School Graduates." Washington, D.C.: Bureau of Statistics, Department of Labor, July 2002.

Watson, C., and Smitherman, G. *Educating African American Males: Detroit's Malcolm X Academy Solution.* Chicago: Third World Press, 1996.

Willis, P. E. *Learning to Labor.* Farmborough, England: Saxon House, 1977.

OBIE CLAYTON *is professor and chair of sociology and director of the Morehouse Research Institute, Morehouse College, Atlanta.*

CYNTHIA LUCAS HEWITT *is assistant professor of sociology at Morehouse College; her focus is political economy, education, and development.*

EDDIE D. GAFFNEY *is dean of student services at Morehouse College.*

2

This chapter surveys the history and theory of men's studies, a field concerned primarily with masculinity and other aspects of men's experience and identity. It argues that men's studies would be an ideal foundation for our work with college men and offers guidelines for programs for men.

Men's Studies as a Foundation for Student Development Work with College Men

Rocco L. Capraro

When the problem of the performance, persistence, and engagement (recall Gar Kellom's Editor's Notes in this volume) of college *women* was first articulated, the academy quickly settled on an explanation: *sexism*. When the problem of the performance, persistence, and engagement of college *persons of color* was first articulated, the academy likewise quickly settled on an explanation: *racism*. But as the problem of the performance, persistence, and engagement of college *men* is being articulated at present, the academy is quickly putting its hands up: *we do not have an explanation*. Why? Essentially, the paradigms of power we used to explain the plight of the relatively powerless in the academy leave us at a loss to explain the plight of the powerful when that plight is not all positive. Or so it seems.

In this chapter, I argue that there is an alternative discourse about men that would help us better understand the experience of college men, and that would serve us well as a foundation for the student development services and programs we offer them: namely, men's studies. I offer, first, a broad outline of the general theory and history of men's studies, and then a discussion of how, conceptually, men's studies might be applied to college men; finally, I present two brief case studies of prevention programs for college men, one on violence and the other on alcohol, with men's studies foundations.

What is men's studies? It is an emerging, interdisciplinary field of knowledge concerned primarily with men's experience, identity, and development throughout the life course. Men's studies focuses on the lives of men, and in particular, on the lives of men as they are framed or made meaningful by prevailing models of what it means to be a man in any particular historical or cultural milieu. Men's studies is best understood as the study of *masculinity* itself; as such, men's studies constitutes a rereading of the texts of men's lives, that is, a second interpretive look at what we know about men viewed through the new lens of masculinity. (Substantial portions of this discussion of men's studies are drawn from Capraro, 2003, with permission.)

In his classic "case for men's studies," Brod defines men's studies as "the study of masculinity as a *specific male* experience, rather than a universal paradigm for *human* experience" (Brod, 1987, pp. 39–40). A brief, representative list of critical topics in men's studies might include boyhood (Pollack, 1998), fathers and fathering (Arendell, 1995), sports (Messner, 1992), the military (Gerzon, 1982), male sexualities (Pronger, 1990), male violence (Berkowitz, 1994), male intimacy (Levinson, 1978), homophobia (Monette, 1992), men of color (Majors and Billson, 1992; Hine and Jenkins, 1999), men in the workplace (Weiss, 1990), men's health (Courtenay, 2000), and theories and histories of masculinity (Brod, 1987; Hearn, 1987; Gilmore, 1990; Kimmel, 1996; Savran, 1998; see also August, 1994). Borrowing from the language of Brod, a "men's studies" of "college men" would be a study of college as a specific male experience rather than as a universal human experience.

Most men's studies scholars and teachers have a values orientation; they regard themselves as engaged in the larger project of "changing men" in response to the problems and uncertainties of a changing world of gender awareness, ideologies, and practices (Kimmel, 1987). Many would regard men's studies as inherently activist. Underlining the solution-seeking aspects of men's studies, Adams and Savran conclude that "perhaps the most desirable goal of scholarship on masculinity would not be the formation of another interdisciplinary field but the radical transformation of its object of study" (Adams and Savran, 2002, p. 7). The activist orientation of men's studies increases its value as a foundation for work with college men.

Historically and conceptually, men's studies is closely related to women's studies and has a great deal in common with that perspective. Women's studies, for the purposes of this chapter, might be understood as a scholarly, and most often feminist, discourse that both derives from and gives shape to the women's movement. The movement had its contemporary origins in Friedan's unmasking of the "feminine mystique," which stipulated that fulfillment as a woman had only one embodiment in late twentieth-century American society: the housewife and mother, who was male-dominated, sexually passive, and maternally nurturing (Friedan, 1963). Women's studies, as the scholarly wing of the women's movement, has as its object of study the female experience, and as its purpose the critique of male-centered ways of knowing and eradication of women's oppression.

In the early 1970s, men responded in a variety of ways to the prospect of change for women in society, pursuing its implications for men. The result was the "men's movement," and *its* intellectual companion, what later came to be called "men's studies." Although the men's movement in general called upon men to be self-reflective about the negative consequences of masculinity—for women and/or for men themselves—and to engage in personal and social change following from a rethinking of masculinity, there were clear ideological divisions within the movement from the start. Conservatives emphasized the disadvantages of being male and validated men as the rightful heads of families and leaders in the public sphere. Mythopoetic men explored men's grief and sought the reconciliation of sons and fathers in their quest for a more confident masculinity that lay buried beneath layers of modernity. The profeminist men's movement argued the virtues of feminism and, in solidarity with the women's movement, committed itself to dismantling sexism (Clatterbaugh, 1990; Capraro, 1994).

Men's studies emerged from the milieu of the 1970s. Men's studies was then, and is now, as diverse as the men's movement itself. We can observe, however, the general evolution of the overall field, up to the present. At first, men's studies was engaged primarily in *consciousness raising* about the perils of the male role and critical thinking about how men are socialized. Even though there has been a significant body of scholarly debate on biological versus social determinants of masculinity, most of men's studies as envisioned in this chapter is decidedly social constructionist.

The introductory essay in David and Brannon's classic text (1976), more than any other single piece of writing, defines the field of men's studies as it was in its early years. The essay, with great explanatory power, succinctly and dramatically identifies four central themes of male socialization (the now legendary watchwords: "no sissy stuff"; "the big wheel"; "the sturdy oak"; and "give 'em hell") and raises a variety of concerns about their consequences, again, for men's and women's lives. Succinctly, men's restricted emotionality, as both agent and consequence of a historically specific, socially constructed masculinity, is the core issue of men's studies as it first emerged (see Randall Ludeman's Chapter Six in this volume).

Two other extremely important, foundational texts from that incunabular period of men's studies are Filene's *Him/Her/Self: Sex Roles in Modern America* (1986) and Pleck's *The Myth of Masculinity* (1981). Filene offers a concise history of the women's movement with an eye toward men's responses to change in women's lives, which in some cases included becoming allies in resisting women's oppression. We learn that masculinity is historical, that our contemporary "crisis of masculinity" is actually a recurring phenomenon, and that men too must rewrite the scripts of their roles if gender justice is to be ultimately achieved.

Pleck rejects the received male sex role identity paradigm in favor of his sex role strain paradigm, which in his view offers a better, more comprehensive account of most men's experience. He demonstrates that traditional masculinity is fraught with "adverse consequences" for men and is also "psychologically dysfunctional" (Pleck, 1981, p. 147). For Pleck, what is most problematic in society is the male role itself and not any individual man having difficulty with that role.

Throughout the 1980s, men's studies texts proliferated. Scholars and teachers in the academy argued successfully for the legitimacy of men's studies as a research field and for the inclusion of men's studies courses and perspectives in curricula. Feminist thought and questions of "theory" acquired a stronger, more explicit, presence in the field; Gramscian concerns about men's *power* and the global and colonialist hegemony of masculinity predominated, particularly among English and Australian men's studies writers and thinkers (Brod and Kaufman, 1994; Brittan, 1989; Connell, 1987, 2000).

Growing scholarly appreciation for the great variety in men's identity and experience also led men's studies to regularize the use of masculinity in the plural (hence, *masculinities)* and to seek closer ties to gay studies and studies of men of color. However, in roughly the same period Robert Bly's mythopoetic "gatherings of men" (1990, 1991) were generating a great deal of curiosity about, and some sympathy for, men, even as they were followed by highly critical responses to Bly and his followers from feminist women and profeminist men (Hagan, 1992).

The result was an increasing consensus in men's studies that neither the story of men as "powerful" nor the story of men as "powerless" alone would provide a thoroughly coherent explanation of men's experience and identity. Depending on one's vantage point, men could appear to be powerful or powerless—in control of, or *not* in control of, their own lives. Consequently, during the 1990s men's studies again conjoins 1970s consciousness of the negative consequences of the male role for men and its 1980s critique of men's power to reexamine in its totality the paradoxical nature of masculinity.

No doubt, the pervasiveness of "postmodern" attention to questions of identity and subjectivity and the disaggregation of human experience in the social sciences also influenced a return to the "paradox of masculinity" in men's studies. In short, it was conceded that *objectively* men as a group may still *have power* over women as a group, but *subjectively* it was observed that many individual men do not *feel powerful.*

Upon closer investigation of the social and psychological mechanisms by which men's lives, and masculinity, are constructed, masculinity was reframed as a shame-based experience. Kimmel (1994), Kaufman (1994), and other men's studies scholars incorporated views on the paradoxical nature of masculinity in their work on the sources of power and pain in men's lives. Kimmel asks, "Why, then, do American men feel so powerless?" He answers, "Because we've constructed the rules of manhood so that only the tiniest fraction of men come to believe they are the biggest of wheels, the sturdiest of oaks, the most virulent repudiators of femininity, the most daring and aggressive" (Kimmel, 1994, p. 138). Even Faludi, who had once published a scorching indictment of antifeminist rhetoric in *Backlash: The Undeclared War Against American Women* (1991), rethought this question in *Stiffed: The Betrayal of the American Man* (1999) and portrayed contemporary men as tragically fallen from a once meaningful masculinity.

Recent scholarship on girls' development viewed from a feminist perspective (Sommers, 2000), studies of "school shootings" widely reported in the media (Garbarino, 1999), and various psychosocial critiques characterizing boyhood as a veritable emotional wasteland (Pollack, 1998) have forcefully raised once again the question of whether boys are advantaged or disadvantaged in contemporary American society. Attention has been drawn to the paradoxical nature of masculinity. Boyhood has become a field of battle where skirmishes over gender are fierce.

Nowhere has the fighting been bloodier than in the arena of education. When boys' persistence, performance, and engagement in school were perceived to be taking a downturn, suspicions arose that the academy had become feminized in the wake of the women's movement. Schools were somehow advantaging girls and women over boys and men. Girls and women in general and feminism in particular were to blame for the unsatisfactory performance of some men and boys. Christina Hoff Sommers, in her provocatively titled book, *The War Against Boys: How Misguided Feminism Is Harming Our Young Men* (2000), traced the downfall of men and boys in the academy to the influence of Carol Gilligan, Mary Pipher, and William Pollack. These three scholars, in Sommers's view, portray girls as the truly needy in a sexist society and boys as pathologized by a toxic traditional masculinity.

The contemporary debate about boys in education is actually a renewal of a larger, recurring debate about boys and boyhood having origins in the Victorian era (Capraro, 2001). Tosh (1999) discusses a virtually inherent tension between "manliness" and "domesticity" in the middle-class home, which historically has driven boys to venture out of the home, away from the discipline of women, into a boyhood of adventure, risk, and violence. To acquire the requisite attributes of manhood, boys must leave women and womanhood behind, even if they are destined one day to return to domesticity in the role of husband and father. Fiedler (1960), in his famous study of *Huckleberry Finn* and other novels, found a similar message deeply embedded in the central literary texts of American culture since the nineteenth century.

Historian E. Anthony Rotundo (1993) observes that in the nineteenth century boys' principal developmental task was disengagement from home. "Male youth culture" made its appearance as the vehicle by which boys would be transported from boyhood to manhood. Male youth culture mediated the conflict between the imperatives of young men's worldly ambition and their psychological needs for attachment. Young men of Rotundo's chosen period gathered together in business districts and colleges; wherever they gathered, a "special culture" developed to support them in a time of need. (Portions of the discussion of Rotundo, Lyman, and shame theory that follows are drawn from Capraro, 2000.)

What about the developmental psychology of college men today, ensconced, as many are away from home in a new learning environment? Lyman's somewhat earlier work (1987) carries us forward from Rotundo's historical analysis, locating college today as a developmental time and place sandwiched between the authority of home and family (during high school) and that of work and family (after graduation). He astutely discloses the *anger* of college men. Lyman characterizes their anger as "latent. . . . about the discipline that middle-class male roles impose upon them, both marriage rules and work rules" (p. 157).

On Lyman's model, college men's great fear is loss of control and powerlessness. Lyman concludes that joking relationships (banter, sexual humor, and so on) among college men facilitate a much-needed connection in men's lives without their having to be self-disclosing or emotionally intimate—that is, with little concomitant vulnerability. This is our contemporary version of Rotundo's boy culture of an earlier period.

For Nuwer (1999), fraternities are emblematic of college men more globally, representing the way men's needs have been provided for in quintessentially traditional college life. Fraternities facilitate a "feeling of belonging" for students who "crave relationships and acceptance" in their college years (p. 38). Unfortunately, they are also the riskiest environments for heavy and problem drinking (Kilmer and others, 1999; Berkowitz and Perkins, 1987). Nationally, just over 80 percent of fraternity residents binge drink, in contrast with the just over 40 percent of all college students who binge (Wechsler and others, 2000). Drinking in fraternities is perhaps best understood as an extreme on a continuum of college men's drinking, dramatizing what may be going on to a lesser extent in traditional student life among a range of men. From the point of view of a needs assessment for college men, we have a great deal to learn and teach from the psychology of brotherhood.

Other research on first-year college men shows their transition to college often involves separation anxiety and loss, followed by grieving. Self-destructive behaviors, including alcohol abuse, are among the significant responses that may manifest some college men's grief (Gold, Neururer, and Miller, 2000).

Rather than seeking a healthy intimacy, Lyman's fraternity men and Gold's first-years look for other ways to manage their emotions, since intimacy (or what creates a need for intimacy) can be shameful. Shame theory advises that to avoid shame boys feel compelled to distance themselves from their mothers (or anything feminine) because of the "considerable discomfort with dependency needs at the level of the peer group" (Krugman, 1995, p. 107). This presents a significant dilemma: boys and men need intimacy, but as long as intimacy is identified with the feminine they reject it.

With Tosh's study in mind, I theorize that most college men perceive programs and services offered by student affairs professionals as a return to "domesticity," in other words as reconstituting their own feminization, *because such programs are inherently nurturing.* They would thus be a source of shame. For that reason, it is suggested by men's studies, college men reject such programs as anathema to their masculinity. By contrast, more stereotypically masculine programs such as athletics or social functions featuring alcohol have few problems filling up with men on most campuses.

"College" today may be like "the home" in history—one of those places where there is tension between the imperatives of manhood and the demands of education. Paradoxically, just when their great college adventure is about to begin, some college men may feel most vulnerable. In short, insidiously and tragically masculinity sabotages programs and services for college men. Ironically, the very programs designed to help them succeed in achieving their educational goals and, in that sense, succeed in achieving the very manhood they were seeking may be rejected.

To be sure, and as is evident in the Morehouse College findings ("Men on Our Campuses," 2001; and Spence and Parikh's Chapter Three in this volume), not all men are equally at risk. African American, Latino, Native American, and very likely Asian and low-income white men are not nearly as successful in college as their higher-income, white counterparts. This means concern for gender and a critique of masculinity alone should not overdetermine the source of all college men's problems with performance, persistence, and engagement. Expressed alternatively, we need to be mindful of the men's studies concept of masculinities, discussed earlier in this chapter, which signifies that there are varieties of men's identities and experiences shaped by multiple factors, among them race, class, sexuality, and religion. Still, insofar as women in virtually all groups are more successful than their male counterparts, gender remains extremely significant for our understanding of men's college success.

Although Lyman himself writes from a secular perspective, current thinking about the role of men's spirituality groups in promoting intimacy among college men suggests that finding new models for promoting male intimacy is important for work with college men (see Chapter Seven, by Longwood, Muesse, and Schipper, in this volume). More generally, and from a men's studies perspective, successful development of student affairs programs and services for men depends on resolving a dilemma: college men need the programs we offer, but their own masculinity severely complicates their subscribing to them.

Here are some suggestions for improving campus environments in a way that facilitates men's studies approaches to work with college men.

1. Create alliances between student affairs professionals who have experience working closely with college men and teaching faculty to develop men's studies courses, or men's studies perspectives in existing

courses. "Alcohol infusion" programs have modeled successful integration of alcohol awareness into curricula. The same could be accomplished with "masculinity" (Perkins and Craig, 2003). Such courses broaden awareness of masculinity among students, faculty, and staff; break down barriers between academic and student affairs; and promote a positive climate in the campus community.

2. Offer speakers and other professional development sessions on men's studies perspectives as part of staff training and campus programming. Develop ways for men to identify the negative consequences of gender role stereotypes in their own lives, such as the various restrictions they face or impose upon themselves as a result of masculinity. A wonderful icebreaker for any workshop for men, for example, is simply to ask the question, "What is difficult about being a man on this campus?" Men often respond with reference to "pressure" or "stress." The group is likely to have a good interaction around that issue as they address the particular content topic, careers, health, study abroad, and so on.

3. Redefine the campus environment as a supportive place that insists on men's taking responsibility for their action but also helps men negotiate the tensions between the imperatives of manhood and the demands of education.

Elsewhere, I have discussed prevention programs for men in the areas of sexual violence (Capraro, 1994) and alcohol (Capraro, 2000), on a foundation of men's studies and from a men's studies perspective. Such programs have in common two critical features: (1) *embedding men's identity, experience, and development in masculinity,* or acknowledging how men live in relation to prevailing models of what it means to be a man; and (2) *employing a male-student-centered pedagogy,* or offering programs that are single-sex, peer-facilitated (by highly trained peers), small-group, interactive, experientially based, residentially based, and required.

The first point highlights the need to explore not just *men* but *masculinity*—in a self-conscious way. Spence and Parikh (Chapter Three in this volume) suggest that although Morehouse historically has emphasized the concept of the "Morehouse Man," contemporary students would benefit from critical perspectives on "manhood" itself. Point two highlights the pedagogic power of the peer group and the necessity of building up learning from men's experience—their "lived lives" as we sometimes express it—rather than preaching down to their minds with rationalist, linear models. In the 1980s, well-intentioned men and women (myself included) concluded that all college men needed for change was a good lecture on feminism and homophobia. Needless to say, that approach was shortsighted.

Following from these two points, alcohol prevention work for men from a men's studies foundation can entail discussion of how alcohol plays a role in the management of men's emotions in a college environment. Unfortunately, drinking remains a "socially acceptable way for men to satisfy their dependency needs while maintaining a social image of independence," even as it masks those needs (Burda and others, 1992, p. 187). Alcohol may be an effective way to cope in the short run, but it is ultimately "self-destructive" (p. 191). In addition, "stress-motivated drinking," or "using alcohol to cope with anxiety and stress," is indeed common in college, but more significantly this reason for drinking becomes "more problematic" in the out years, after graduation, as measured by negative consequences on the individual (Perkins, 1999, p. 225).

4. For virtually any kind of workshop with men, raise the issue of male intimacy, or male-male relations in a particular community. Begin by grounding what follows in men's own experience. For alcohol prevention work with fraternity men, for example, begin by asking a question (or having them free-write) on the topic, "Why I Joined a Fraternity." Usually, brothers respond with a reference to friendship or unconditional support and acceptance. From there, move to the question of the gendered nature of those relationships and needs, and from there to the question of the role of alcohol in male intimacy.

5. Prevention work on sexual violence likewise should help men understand the relationship between masculinity and violence. Ask men, individually and collectively, not to be paralyzed in guilt but to take responsibility for their actions. On my own campus, our sexual assault prevention program for men employs the pedagogy articulated earlier in this chapter (Berkowitz, 1994). That program (and programs based on the model) has been shown to effect change in a positive direction in the attitudes and values associated with the perpetration of sexual assault by men (Berkowitz, 2002). Although empathy induction is important for consciousness raising, focus instead on the male socialization that itself puts men at risk to perpetrate sexual assault. A single-sex workshop helps maintain this focus.

6. Contrary to what is often heard, required student affairs programs can be effective. On our campus, they receive positive evaluations from male participants, so require programs with confidence. Finally, homegrown scenarios drawn from student life on your own campus result in more complex and engaged discussion than the videos produced by outside agencies.

Whatever the specific approach, each program should rest on the assumption that if college men understand why their lives are not working—why they are not achieving their educational goals—they will come to see the part masculinity plays in their experience. Making this known to college men is the virtue of men's studies as a foundation for our work with them, and it is why performance, persistence, and engagement of college men is likely to improve once programs are built on that foundation.

References

Adams, R., and Savran, D. "Introduction." In R. Adams and D. Savran (eds.), *The Masculinity Studies Reader*. Malden, Mass.: Blackwell, 2002.

Arendell, T. *Fathers and Divorce*. Thousand Oaks, Calif.: Sage, 1995.

August, E. R. *The New Men's Studies: A Selected and Annotated Interdisciplinary Bibliography* (2nd ed.). Englewood, Colo.: Libraries Unlimited, 1994.

Berkowitz, A. (ed.). *Men and Rape: Theory, Research, and Prevention Programs in Higher Education.* San Francisco: Jossey-Bass, 1994.

Berkowitz, A. "Fostering Men's Responsibility for Preventing Sexual Assault." In P. A. Schewe (ed.), *Preventing Violence in Relationships.* Washington, D.C.: American Psychological Association, 2002.

Berkowitz, A., and Perkins, H. W. "Recent Research on Gender Differences in Collegiate Alcohol Use." *Journal of American College Health,* 1987, *36,* 123–129.

Bly, R. *Iron John: A Book About Men.* Reading, Mass.: Addison-Wesley, 1990.

Bly, R. "What Men Really Want." In K. Thompson (ed.), *To Be a Man: In Search of the Deep Masculine.* Los Angeles: Tarcher, 1991.

Brittan, A. *Masculinity and Power.* Oxford, U.K.: Basil Blackwell, 1989.

Brod, H. "The Case for Men's Studies." In H. Brod (ed.), *The Making of Masculinities: The New Men's Studies.* Boston: Allen and Unwin, 1987.

Brod, H., and Kaufman, M. *Theorizing Masculinities.* Thousand Oaks, Calif.: Sage, 1994.

Burda, P. C., Tushup, R. J., and Hackman, P. S. "Masculinity and Social Support in Alcoholic Men." *Journal of Men's Studies,* 1992, *1*(2), 187–193.

Capraro, R. L. "Disconnected Lives: Men, Masculinity, and Rape Prevention." In A. D. Berkowitz (ed.), *Men and Rape: Theory, Research, and Prevention Programs in Higher Education.* San Francisco: Jossey-Bass, 1994.

Capraro, R. L. "Why College Men Drink: Alcohol, Adventure, and the Paradox of Masculinity." *Journal of American College Health,* 2000, *48*(6), 307–315.

Capraro, R. L. "Feminism and the Preservation of a Sentimental Boyhood: A Response to Sommers and Garbarino." Unpublished paper, Wagner College lecture series on boys, 2001.

Capraro, R. L. "Men's Studies." In M. Kimmel (ed.), *Men and Masculinities: A Social, Cultural, and Historical Encyclopedia.* Santa Barbara, Calif.: ABC-CLIO, 2003.

Clatterbaugh, K. *Contemporary Perspectives on Masculinity: Men, Women, and Politics in Modern Society.* Boulder, Colo.: Westview Press, 1990.

Connell, R. W. *Gender and Power.* Stanford, Calif.: Stanford University Press, 1987.

Connell, R. W. *The Men and the Boys.* Berkeley: University of California Press, 2000.

David, D. S., and Brannon, R. "The Male Sex Role: Our Culture's Blueprint of Manhood and What It's Done for Us Lately." In *The Forty-Nine Percent Majority: The Male Sex Role.* New York: Random House, 1976.

Faludi, S. *Backlash: The Undeclared War Against American Women.* New York: Crown, 1991.

Faludi, S. *Stiffed: The Betrayal of the American Man.* New York: Morrow, 1999.

Fiedler, L. *Love and Death in the American Novel.* Scranton, Pa.: Criterion Books, 1960.

Filene, P. G. *Him/Her/Self: Sex Roles in Modern America* (2nd ed.). Baltimore, Md.: Johns Hopkins University Press, 1986.

Friedan, B. *The Feminine Mystique.* New York: Norton, 1963.

Garbarino, J. *Lost Boys: Why Our Sons Turn Violent and How We Can Save Them.* New York: Anchor Books, 1999.

Gerzon, M. *Choice of Heroes: The Changing Face of American Manhood.* Boston: Houghton Mifflin, 1982.

Gilmore, D. D. *Manhood in the Making: Cultural Concepts of Masculinity.* New Haven, Conn.: Yale University Press, 1990.

Gold, J., Neururer, J., and Miller, M. "Disenfranchised Grief Among First-Semester Male University Students: Implications for Systemic and Individual Interventions." *Journal of the First Year Experience,* 2000, *12*(1), 7–27.

Hagan, K. L. (ed.). *Women Respond to the Men's Movement: A Feminist Collection.* San Francisco: Harper San Francisco, 1992.

Hearn, J. *The Gender of Oppression: Men, Masculinity, and the Critique of Marxism.* New York: St. Martin's Press, 1987.

Hine, D. C., and Jenkins, E. (eds.). *A Question of Manhood: A Reader in U.S. Black Men's History and Masculinity.* Bloomington: Indiana University Press, 1999.

Journal of American College Health, 2000, 48(6) [Special issue edited by W. H. Courtenay].

Kaufman, M., and Kimmel, M. (eds.). *Theorizing Masculinities.* Thousand Oaks, Calif.: Sage, 1994.

Kilmer, J. R., and others. "Liability Management or Risk Management? Evaluation of a Greek System Alcohol Policy." *Psychology of Addictive Behaviors,* 1999, 13(4), 269–278.

Kimmel, M. (ed.). *Changing Men: New Directions in Research on Men and Masculinity.* Thousand Oaks, Calif.: Sage, 1987.

Kimmel, M. "Masculinity as Homophobia: Fear, Shame, and Silence in the Construction of Gender Identity." In H. Brod and M. Kaufman (eds.), *Theorizing Masculinities.* Thousand Oaks, Calif.: Sage, 1994.

Kimmel, M. *Manhood in America: A Cultural History.* New York: Free Press, 1996.

Kimmel, M. S., and Messner, M. A. (eds.). *Men's Lives* (5th ed.). Boston: Allyn and Bacon, 2001.

Krugman, S. "Male Development and the Transformation of Shame." In Levant, R. F., and Pollack, W. S. (eds.), *A New Psychology of Men.* New York: Basic, 1995.

Levinson, D. J. *The Seasons of a Man's Life.* New York: Ballantine Books, 1978.

Lyman, P. "The Fraternal Bond as a Joking Relationship." In M. S. Kimmel (ed.), *Changing Men: New Directions in Research on Men and Masculinity.* Thousand Oaks, Calif.: Sage, 1987.

Majors, R., and Billson, J. M. *Cool Pose: The Dilemmas of Black Manhood in America.* New York: Simon and Schuster, 1992.

"Men on Our Campuses: A Summary Report from 'Reconnecting Males to Liberal Education,' a Morehouse College Symposium." April 2001, Atlanta.

Messner, M. A. *Power at Play: Sports and the Problem of Masculinity.* Boston: Beacon Press, 1992.

Monette, P. *Becoming a Man: Half a Life Story.* San Francisco: Harper San Francisco, 1992.

Nuwer, H. *Wrongs of Passage: Fraternities, Sororities, Hazing, and Binge Drinking.* Bloomington: Indiana University Press, 1999.

Perkins, H. W. "Stress-Motivated Drinking in Collegiate and Postcollegiate Young Adulthood: Life Course and Gender Patterns." *Journal of Studies on Alcohol,* 1999, 60(2), 219–227.

Perkins, H. W., and Craig, D. W. "The Hobart and William Smith Colleges Experiment: A Synergistic Social Norms Approach Using Print, Electronic Media, and Curriculum Infusion to Reduce Collegiate Problem Drinking." In Perkins, H. W. (ed.), *The Social Norms Approach to Preventing School and College Age Substance Abuse.* San Francisco: Jossey-Bass, 2003.

Pleck, J. *The Myth of Masculinity.* Cambridge, Mass.: MIT Press, 1981.

Pollack, W. *Real Boys: Rescuing Our Sons from the Myths of Boyhood.* New York: Holt, 1998.

Pronger, B. *The Arena of Masculinity: Sports, Homosexuality, and the Meaning of Sex.* New York: St. Martin's Press, 1990.

Rotundo, E. A. *American Manhood: Transformations in Masculinity from the Revolution to the Present.* New York: Basic Books, 1993.

Savran, D. *Taking It Like a Man: White Masculinity, Masochism, and Contemporary American Culture.* Princeton, N.J.: Princeton University Press, 1998.

Sommers, C. H. *The War Against Boys: How Misguided Feminism Is Harming Our Young Men.* New York: Simon and Schuster, 2000.

Tosh, J. *A Man's Place: Masculinity and the Middle-Class Home in Victorian England.* New Haven: Yale University Press, 1999.

Wechsler, H., and others. "What Colleges Are Doing about Student Binge Dinking: A Survey of College Administrators." *Journal of American College Health,* 2000, 48(10) 219–226.

Weiss, R. S. *Staying the Course: The Social and Emotional Lives of Men Who Do Well at Work.* New York: Fawcett Columbine, 1990.

ROCCO L. CAPRARO received his Ph.D. from Washington University and is associate dean of Hobart College (Geneva, New York), where he directs Rape Prevention Education for Men and coordinates the men's studies minor.

3

This chapter looks at education of college men in a single-sex learning environment from the perspective of a woman's college.

A Women's College Perspective on the Education of College Men

Cynthia Neal Spence, Manju Parikh

The education of college men assumes special significance in the context of single-sex male institutions. The rarity of these institutions furnishes a unique opportunity to look at what works for men, but when these institutions are also in partnerships with women's colleges there is an opportunity to look at what works for educating men and women together. This chapter analyzes the education of college men at Morehouse from the perspective of Spelman, a women's college. It also addresses the question of preparing the young male leaders of tomorrow: what has women's studies got to do with it?

Morehouse and Spelman (Cynthia Neal Spence)

Morehouse College was founded in 1867 in Augusta, Georgia, just two years after the end of the Civil War. The history of the founding of Morehouse College is not remarkably different from the founding of other historically black institutions of higher education, except that the institution was founded as a single-sex institution for men. Fourteen years after the founding of Morehouse College, Spelman College was founded in 1881. These two institutions' shared missions, close physical proximity, and history of formal and informal professional and personal alliances suggest that the two offer environments that are complementary. The interactions among faculty, staff, and students might suggest that some common themes shape and frame the educational experiences of the young men and women who matriculate at these two institutions.[1] One shared emphasis has historically been on the "uplift of the race." This emphasis on racial uplift was more apparent within the culture of Morehouse College because of its status as a male institution. The goal of "race men" is inextricably linked to the discourse on leadership development of the Morehouse Man. Both Spelman and Morehouse have emphasized the need for their graduates to participate as change agents and leaders for their communities. Spelman College continues to introduce varied models of the "Spelman Woman."[2]

To understand how Morehouse College views its historical and current mission, one must understand the intentionality associated with distinguishing the Morehouse Man from other men, particularly men of African descent. Past and present presidents of Morehouse College have alluded to the unique opportunities presented by leading an institution with a primary mission of educating men of African American and African descent. This captive audience would be prepared to rise above the masses and take their rightful places of leadership. In some ways, Morehouse College and Spelman College are viewed by many as the personification of W.E.B. Du Bois's notion of the "talented tenth." Both institutions have historically boasted that they enrolled the best and the brightest of the African American communities across this country. This was particularly true prior to desegregation, because of the limited higher education options for African American students. These themes of racial uplift and development of the talented tenth continue to frame much of the formal and informal curricular and cocurricular discussion about how to best prepare these students for the world that awaits them beyond the baccalaureate degree.

This chapter examines the education of Morehouse men to answer a more general question about the prevailing ideological perspectives that shape the education of men. A secondary question is how such dominant frameworks prepare men for personal and professional growth in diverse environments that require sensitivity as well as respect and appreciation for differences on the basis of race, ethnicity, gender, sexuality, religion, privilege, and other human characteristics that distinguish one from another. From a women's college perspective, a particular focus is how the education of men in a single-sex environment parallels the education of women in a single-sex environment. In this case the focus is on how a Spelman educational paradigm might frame questions about the core of the educational experience of Morehouse men.

Frances A. Maher and Mary Kay Thompson Tetreault (2001) examine the dynamics of classroom pedagogy in their text *The Feminist Classroom*. Of particular interest to the authors was how classroom dynamics change or evolve when the pedagogy is woman-centered and taught from a feminist perspective. It is acknowledged that women-centered discourses do not necessarily employ feminist theoretical perspectives. For purposes of this research, the questions become, How do classroom dynamics change or evolve when the pedagogy is male-centered? Or should one assume that the opposite of a woman-centered or feminist classroom is one that is framed by notions of masculinity?[3]

These questions force an analysis of how the student body shapes and informs the curricular and cocurricular experiences of faculty, students, and staff at single-sex institutions. Does the fact that an institution is all-male presume that "men's studies" does (or should) frame academic discourse?

In *Manhood in America* (1996) Michael Kimmel speaks to the reality that in the absence of women's studies one does not necessarily have a counter correlate of men's studies. Although the text and the subject matter may be dominated by male presence, it does not necessarily result in a pedagogy that is comparable to a feminist or woman-centered pedagogy. Just as a woman-centered pedagogy may not be necessarily feminist, a male-centered pedagogy may not necessarily be based on men's studies. A pedagogy framed by men's studies focuses on the experiences of being men. Emphasis is placed on how diverse conceptions and social constructions of manhood have informed the text and the experiences of men.

Literature on Morehouse College speaks explicitly about the Morehouse Man as if there is an identifiable construct that neatly fits this description. Like Spelman College, the Spelman Woman construct becomes an idealized monolithic image of womanhood.

Is it possible to educate men to become world leaders without focusing specifically on the diversity of male images that they themselves represent and how these images are reflected in the larger society? What has long been assumed by women's colleges is that in order to empower and prepare women to assume positions of leadership and self-direction in the public and private spheres, they must not only be exposed to images of women's empowerment but also gain greater understanding of themselves and how various social constructions of gender have defined and restricted their roles in society and continue to do so. Thus, from a women's college perspective it is assumed that an education grounded in engaging male students in similar discursive exercises would be an analogous and necessary experience.

As Morehouse College continues to prepare its students for their "rightful place" in society, it is engaging in a review of the current core curriculum. The standard liberal arts curriculum places special emphasis on racial and cultural diversity. The core curriculum has been paired with a student development model that frames the curricular and cocurricular experience of Morehouse students. The development of intellectual competencies in the liberal arts through the core curricular experience and the major experience is framed by an expectation that the curricular programs will "empower students by fostering high expectations and habits for independent learning."

Willis Sheftall, Morehouse College provost, shared in a recent interview that the college has recognized a need to more intentionally address issues of masculinity and self-definition through curricular and cocurricular experiences. Sheftall candidly acknowledged that because male domination has been a dominant paradigm in society, the concept of "maleness" as a separate issue has not been adequately addressed by Morehouse College. This recognition is not surprising given that society has not felt a need to interrogate maleness as a gender construct in the same ways that femaleness has been the subject of analysis and, more recently, deconstruction and reconstruction.

Morehouse College will begin to focus more on engaging young men in curricular and cocurricular experiences that examine maleness as a social construct that can be represented in varied ways.[4] Many feminist scholars would argue that predominant social constructions of gender have not acknowledged or allowed representation of diverse models of womanhood or manhood. Monolithic conceptions of masculinity and femininity that favor traditional notions of what it means to be a man and a woman have shaped and framed socialization experiences of males and females. These binary conceptions of gender have allowed little room for within-group difference. Such narrow constructions of masculinity often foster and nurture attitudes and behaviors that are homophobic or hypermasculine. Morehouse College's strategic attentiveness to the development of broader conceptions and demonstrations of the performance of masculinity will engage students in curricular and cocurricular activities that should permit multitextured analysis of the social construction of masculinity.

A women's college perspective strongly supports creation of safe spaces for men to discuss and express how societal and institutional notions of manhood can in some instances encourage quite negative manifestations of masculinity. This subtext is fueled by the reality that homosocial environments sometimes breed unhealthy expressions of masculinity.[5] Kimmell asserts that "masculinity defined through homosocial interaction contains many parts, including the camaraderie, fellowship, and intimacy often celebrated in male culture. It also includes homophobia" (1996, p. 8). Kimmel explains that his definition of homophobia is not just an irrational fear of homosexuals or the fear of being perceived as gay. Homophobia, according to Kimmel, also includes a fear that other men will suggest that one does not measure up to some known and accepted concept or standard of a "real man" (p. 8).

It is suggested that men's colleges might want to rethink how they conceptualize the curriculum and cocurriculum for male students. If women's colleges both empower women students (preparing them to assume positions of leadership and self-direction) and give them greater understanding of themselves and how various social constructions of gender have defined and restricted their roles in society and continue to do so, then it is not enough for men's colleges to just empower male students (similarly preparing them to assume positions of leadership) without also affording them the same kind of greater understanding of themselves and social constructions of gender. This is the challenge for men's institutions.

Although Morehouse College has not adopted a men's studies concentration as some other institutions have, the development of courses with specific focuses on men's studies is not discouraged. Such a curricular focus would offer, in a male-centered environment, an opportunity to examine and interrogate their concepts of masculinity and the multifaceted reality of men's lives and experiences. Classroom discussions would and should foster open dialogue and debate around conceptions of masculinity. Such a curriculum would perhaps do what the work of Rudolph Byrd and Beverly Guy-Sheftall (2001) does in their edited volume *Traps: African American Men on Gender and Sexuality* to expose the writings of African American male literary and political leaders on the subject of gender and sexuality. This text offers a broad view of the writings and thoughts of such men as W.E.B. Du Bois, Frederick Douglass, and Benjamin E. Mays, great men who are justifiably elevated to role model and mentor status for Morehouse men. These men were progressive about the performance of masculinity, as well as holding prowoman and profeminist views.[6] Revered leaders, they acknowledged that leadership takes many forms and that it must recognize and embrace the value of differing perspectives and approaches to leadership.

The historical and contemporary story of Morehouse College is full of references to the development of African American male leaders. In early years, this development focused on preparing leaders for local and national communities. In 2004, it is rare to hear such a limited geographical scope for Morehouse men; the expectation is that they will be prepared to take the mantle of leadership in the world community.

In a recent interview with Walter Fluker, director of the Morehouse College Leadership Institute, it was clear that his emphasis on leadership development and training follows a more progressive nontraditional leadership model that focuses on developing the outer and inner core of the leader. This model recognizes that different characteristics are required for the role of the twenty-first-century leader in a diverse society. Traditional leadership programs within and outside of the higher education community often focus more on visible signs of leadership such as personal presentation skills, including public speaking and personal deportment, problem solving, and argumentation. These visible skills have been emphasized as a way to ensure that a Morehouse man's presence is always known.

Mona Phillips, professor of sociology at Spelman College, speaks specifically to her observation that Morehouse men quite comfortably gravitate to the center of the discourse or public arena.[7] Her assessment is that this reality is fueled by an institutional discourse that suggests that "Morehouse men" should always assume center stage. A much quoted quip is that "you can always tell a Morehouse Man, but you can't tell him much." This speaks to the notion or perception of the Morehouse Man always asserting himself as the authority in any given situation.

One must be able to contextualize the need to project this image within the sociohistorical context of the experiences of African American males.

Such an emphasis on empowerment within this male institution is grounded by the reality of institutionalized disenfranchisement of African American males in various sectors of society. Discussion of historical disenfranchisement of African Americans is often male-centered.

Phillips suggests that emphasis should also be placed on the need for males to decenter themselves and develop better listening and reflection skills. In contrast, she acknowledges that women students must be encouraged to find their voices, move to the center and away from the margins, and take their rightful place as leaders. Perhaps the reality is that both institutions emphasize that their students need to gravitate to the center because societal constructs that are gendered and racialized do not naturally acknowledge the presence of African American leadership that does not conform to white male patriarchal structures. Race and gender inform faculty and staff at the women's and men's institutions in ways that often suggest that a hierarchy must always be the norm. Sometimes male leadership models in this context become contorted and do not acknowledge that both male and female leaders can coexist in environments that readily accept and respect the contributions of both genders. The particular situation of Morehouse and Spelman Colleges is unique in that their social location as historically black institutions informs the need for leadership development in some ways that might not exist at historically white institutions.

Historically, the preparation of the Morehouse Man has called upon delivery of a certain select skill set that enables him to assume his rightful place of leadership within both the public and private spheres. One should not minimize the significance of this level of preparation. However, overemphasis on the outward signs of leadership may create a vessel without the necessary substance to sustain its survival. Fluker speaks specifically to what he characterizes as the need to focus on the "inner life of the leader." This focus reflects attention to what he calls "soft skills." Skills that introduce values such as integrity, ethical decision making, empathy, humility, and moral reasoning are quite intentionally and strategically inserted into the leadership development curriculum under Fluker's direction. He acknowledged that an emphasis on developing soft skills might have initially been perceived as antithetical to the model of leadership espoused for Morehouse men. The "Man" in Morehouse is not to be publicly perceived as soft. Carol Gilligan's "different voice" theory (1982) suggests that these characteristics are seen as "feminine" traits. The public perception of Morehouse has not lent itself to the reality that just as there are diverse leadership models, there are diverse skills that must be considered as we prepare for leadership in the twenty-first century.

What is clear from this limited analysis is that one of the prevailing ideologies shaping the education of men at Morehouse College focuses on cultivation of the Morehouse Man as a leader in all arenas. This leadership emphasis continues to be framed by an agenda of "racial uplift." Classroom and outside experiences are framed by this intention to equip students with the necessary skills to succeed as leaders. Certainly a single chapter does not afford an opportunity to fully engage this topic of the education of males; the complexities around such a provocative topic cannot be fully exposed and investigated. To suggest that there is even one woman's college perspective does not do justice to such a multitextured analysis. From a woman's college perspective, it is important that the messages communicated to Morehouse men include the reality that the unique position of a single-sex male institution poses an exceptional opportunity to create various positive narratives on masculinity and male leadership. The single-narrative approach is limiting to the institution and to the students who matriculate. The models of leadership that include a mixture of traditional notions of public leadership and nontraditional notions associated with the concept of ethical leadership are critical to the survival of all those called upon to lead. The insidious nature of discrimination on the basis of race, ethnicity, gender, sexuality, religion, and ability (among other personal and social identifiers) continues to require all institutions of higher education to focus more specifically on issues of difference and diversity within and outside of group membership.

Preparing the Young Male Leaders of Tomorrow: What Has Women's Studies Got to Do with It? (Manju Parikh)

Not unlike the relationship of Morehouse and Spelman Colleges, Saint John's University and the College of Saint Benedict are two distinct liberal arts institutions with a uniquely defined coordinate relationship. The two residential campuses are five miles apart, but their curriculum and academic departments are joint and students can take classes on either campus, with buses regularly transporting the students to and fro.

In 1994 the faculty at the two institutions decided to establish a new minor in women's studies because they felt there was a need for a more comprehensive and systemic study of gender. A few male colleagues advocated a parallel men's studies program, which would help introduce gender study of men and masculinities. However, there were not enough courses for this separate minor; a compromise solution was a joint gender and women's studies minor with the understanding that in the future more men's studies courses will be developed and added to the program.

In these ten years, the minor has grown considerably, resulting in a significant enrichment of the liberal arts curriculum. Most remarkable has been the promotion of gender awareness through extracurricular programming in partnership with the Office of Student Development on the two campuses, cemented by the Learning Communities Initiative.

As may be expected, development of the minor has been accompanied with certain difficult dilemmas and tensions. In the early years, the minor not only emphasized the cultural and social construction of gender but also privileged women's gender development. For example, the catalog described the Introduction to Gender and Women's Studies course in this way: "the course explores the social construction of gender, and how race, class, ethnicity, and sexual orientation construct women's experiences and identities. Students will read a variety of feminist scholarship, as well as explore current debates within the discipline."

Thus the introductory course was designed to enhance gender awareness of women students through a critical examination of a variety of societal norms and historical practices institutionalizing women's oppression. However, others who wanted the introductory course to be more inclusive (that is, deal with biological construction of gender differences as well as the gendered socialization of men) felt frustrated by the exclusion of their viewpoints.

Such tensions are real and reflect the likely challenges to be faced by any joint program. For the advocates of women's studies, creation of the GWST minor was a long-awaited acknowledgment of the feminist critique of the curriculum. The new minor would finally allow them to reorient the curriculum, enabling a focus on women's experiences, concerns, and contributions. From their point of view, it was unreasonable to expect the Introductory Gender and Women's Studies course to focus extensively on men's issues, although they were prepared to support new men's studies courses dealing with men's concerns in the GWST minor. However, men's studies courses did not attract enough students, which caused friction with enrollment-sensitive administrators. The dilemma of inclusion of men's gender concerns in women's studies courses has remained a thorny issue.

It is important to acknowledge that in the intervening ten years the orientation of the GWST minor has changed considerably. A new introductory course called Studies in Masculinities has been designed and offered a few times.

The description of the GWST minor was also revised to be more inclusive, acknowledging "a pluralism of theoretical approaches, emphasizing the intersections between gender, sexuality, race, class, ethnicity, and nationality." Furthermore, a spring 2002 workshop on Integrating Men's Studies into Women's Studies courses, with Chris Kilmartin, and a summer workshop in August 2002 offered valuable support for several introductory courses.

After the workshop, a steering committee established several new guidelines accepting that all "GWST Intro courses will address the *gender concerns of both women and men*" (emphasis added), and that the intro courses would include information about the U.S. women's movements, including those of minority women, and information on ways in which the men's movement and GLBT (gay, lesbian, bisexual and transgender) movement are theoretically and historically related to the women's movement and how they operate independently now.

A review of the syllabi of the GWST intro courses since fall 2002 reflects the integration of the materials from men's studies, women's studies, and

GLBT studies, but the underlying disagreements remain; the dialogue about different focuses and interests appears to continue. Many women's studies advocates, who genuinely support redefinition of traditional masculinity through the new gender study of men, still feel reluctant to embrace and share the burden of promoting male gender awareness and mentoring in women's studies courses. This task, from their perspective, would be best handled by male colleagues in men's studies courses.

I count myself among the advocates of women's studies; however, I favor integrating research from men's studies into women's studies courses. My advocacy stems from practical considerations, a theoretical critique against essentialist feminism, my philosophical values, and political and strategic concerns. I also speak from the direct experience of having taught the Intro to Gender and Women's Studies in an integrated format with Charles Thornbury in fall 2000, when our students repeatedly expressed their appreciation of the inclusive curriculum.

Why do I favor such integration? First, it helps to reach, and connect with, both women and men in our classes. Analysis of student enrollment data of GWST 101, Introduction to Gender and Women's Studies, shows a persistent trend of majority women and a small minority of men students. Even the other introductory course, GWST 103, Studies in Masculinity, attracted more women than men students. The majority of the GWST elective courses also show the same pattern of greater enrollment of women than men.

It has been suggested that instead of perceiving men who are enrolled in the Introduction to Women's Studies classes as a barrier to creation of an exclusive "women's space," one might welcome their presence as "an educational opportunity [as opposed to a burden] for positive feminist engagement" (Hughes, 1999, p. 75). If the intro class instructor wishes to encourage men to engage with feminism productively, then the instructor would need to treat the men as active "members of the class by forming coalition out of something that everyone can participate in, i.e., the critique of dismantling [all kinds of] privilege" (p. 84).

In the 1980s, women of color (African American, Hispanic, and Asian as well as Third World feminists) seriously challenged the "universalist" and "essentialist" theoretical assumptions of U.S. feminism, which were in fact based on the experiences of white middle-class women (Boca Zinn and Dill, 1966). However, if the feminist goal is to oppose all systems of domination (that is, on the basis of gender, race, class, sexuality, or any other form of privilege), then it might be better to adopt a teaching method more inclusive of women's varied experiences and rethink the essentialist pedagogical approach, even vis-à-vis men (Hughes, 1999).

Another way to reflect on the issue is to ask whether it is necessary to "essentialize" men to build solidarity against the gendered oppression of women. For me, there are some ethical and philosophical considerations involved here. Imagine a class where the theme of the discussion is violence against women. The discussion involves acknowledgment of widespread violence experienced by women worldwide; it involves acknowledging that men commit 90 percent of these violent acts. However, in this context an important caveat also needs to be mentioned: although "aggression is deeply embedded within traditional masculinity, it is important to remember that *most men are not violent*" (Kilmartin, 2000, p. 239; emphasis added). Is it fair to brush with one stroke all members of a group for acts committed by a small minority? On an ethical basis, most of us would object to a stereotyped remark about predatory sexual conduct of men from a racial minority, but this same ethical principle is not recalled when generalizations are made about the behavior of all men.

Currently many profeminist men are engaged in a serious reflection of their responsibility for the aggression and discrimination experienced by women in society, by arguing that "men should acknowledge the way in which their identity is tied to patriarchy. . . . [and to advocate] a feminist-based male identity politics. . . . not just for improving men's lives but [also] changing structures of power to end the oppression of women and children as well as to aid resistance to other forms of oppression in the culture" (Jensen, 1998, p. 32).

Another possible way for feminists to deal with this issue is to recast their argument and appeal to men as morally and ethically guided beings who should support the agenda of ending women's oppression. Instead of assuming their opposition, we might win allies in the struggle (Johnson, 1997, 2003). Many scholars in men's studies are deeply engaged in redefining traditional masculinity. This is one agenda that would be mutually beneficial; therefore it is very much in women's interest to support it.

Finally, let me address the political aspect of the issue, which connects the last strand in my argument for integrating men's studies into the women's studies curriculum. At a time in our history when, in a concerted plan to resurrect hegemonic masculinity, young men are being wooed by right-wing narratives of "victimhood" through attacks on affirmative action by mischaracterizing the project for racial and gender equality, can women afford to miss the opportunity to seek the "hearts and minds" of these young men for the agenda of gender justice? If the goal is to achieve more progress in the next few decades, then men must be equally engaged in the struggle for gender justice—in other words, play a vital role as strategic allies. In sum, to cement our shared interests, I advocate that men's studies be incorporated into the women's studies curriculum. If we integrate the curriculum, more young men will be inclined to take these courses and gain a better awareness of their own gendered selves and of gender-based oppression. This knowledge can only lead to making such young men better leaders, colleagues, and partners in the future.

Notes

1. Spelman and Morehouse Colleges are members of the Atlanta University Center Complex. Spelman College enrolls approximately two thousand students, and Morehouse College approximately three thousand. The physical proximity of the two

institutions (literally within a city block of each other) results in significant exchange among students in classes, student organizations, and social events.

2. A soon to be published text by Harry Lefever, professor of sociology, focuses on the role of Spelman women in the civil rights movement. A recent publication by Cynthia Griggs Fleming (1998) on the life of Spelman alumna Ruby Doris Smith, entitled *Soon We Will Not Cry,* is another example of Spelman women being identified as active agents of social change for the uplift of the race.

3. One common theme among women's colleges is placing women at the center of disciplinary inquiry. Although not all pedagogy would necessarily be considered feminist pedagogy, women's empowerment and representation in all arenas is consistently emphasized. At Spelman College the context is further expanded to focus on the lives of women of color. Various representations of women are presented. Leadership models are often framed by a discussion of servant leadership denoting the expectation that leaders become a part of their community through service and active engagement with members of the community.

4. Sheftall shared a copy of the Morehouse College "Student Development Model and the General Education Program at Morehouse College: Goals, Student Learning Outcomes, and Outcome Indicators"; draft, Nov. 24, 2003.

5. The relationships between Spelman College and Morehouse College have been overwhelmingly positive; however, incidents of intimate interpersonal violence have been characteristic of some relationships between Morehouse men and Spelman women. In addition, the presence of homophobia on both campuses continues to concern faculty, staff, and administrators. The nature of single-sex institutions often fuels greater need, particularly among men, to "overexaggerate their masculinity—hypermasculinity, in order not to be considered gay." During the 2002–03 academic year, a tragic incident of aggravated assault occurred when one Morehouse man believed that a male he suspected of being gay was subjecting him to an unprovoked flirtation. The Morehouse student was subsequently expelled, tried, and convicted on a charge of aggravated assault and sentenced to ten years in prison. Both the perpetrator and victim will never be the same.

6. *Traps* introduces the reader to the speeches of Frederick Douglass on the imperative of women's right to vote. He is specifically quoted as stating that men should be willing to recognize that women have the same rights as men and that men should not assume positions of obstruction (Byrd and Guy-Sheftall, 2001). The work of W.E.B. Du Bois is also cited, with particular attention to his belief that the uplift of women was as significant as the need to address the issues presented by the problem of the twentieth century being that of the color line. In the "Damnation of Women," Du Bois states that "the uplift of women is, next to the problem of the color line and the peace movement, our greatest modern cause" (Byrd and Guy-Sheftall, 2001, p. 67). Throughout the selected writing of Benjamin Elijah Mays are many of his references that do not support acceptance of stereotypical models of masculinity based on aggressive or hypermasculine behavior.

7. Phillips is quoted extensively in Maher and Tetreault's *The Feminist Classroom* (2001). Phillips speaks specifically about how a feminist perspective guides her teaching and nonteaching interactions with students.

References

Boca Zinn, M., and Dill, B. T. "Theorizing Difference from Multiracial Feminism." *Feminist Studies,* 1966, 22(2), 321–332.

Byrd, R., and Guy-Sheftall, B. *Traps: African American Men on Gender and Sexuality.* Bloomington: Indiana University Press, 2001.

Fleming, C. G. *Soon We Will Not Cry: The Liberation of Ruby Doris Smith.* Lanham, Md.: Rowman and Littlefield, 1998.

Gilligan, C. *A Different Voice: Psychological Theory and Women's Development.* Cambridge, Mass.: Harvard University Press, 1982.

Hughes G. "Revisiting the 'Men Problem' in Introductory Women's Studies Classes." In B. Scott Winkler and C. Di Palma (eds.), *Teaching Introduction to Women's Studies.* New York: Bergin and Garvey, 1999.

Jensen, R. "Men's Lives and Feminist Theory." In K. Conway-Turner (ed.), *Women's Studies in Transition: The Pursuit of Interdisciplinarity.* Cranbury, N.J.: Associated University Press, 1998.

Johnson, A. *Gender Knot: Unraveling Our Patriarchal Legacy.* Philadelphia: Temple University Press, 1997.

Johnson, A. "The Struggle for Gender Equality Doesn't Have to Be a Battle." Public lecture, Men's Lives and Women's Lives Lecture Series, Saint John's University, Collegeville, Minn., Jan. 29, 2003.

Kilmartin, C. *The Masculine Self* (2nd ed.). New York: McGraw-Hill, 2000.

Kimmel, M. *Manhood in America: A Cultural History.* New York: Free Press, 1996.

Maher, F. A., and Thompson Tetreault, M. K. *The Feminist Classroom: Dynamics of Gender, Race, and Privilege.* Lanham, Md.: Rowman and Littlefield, 2001.

CYNTHIA NEAL SPENCE *is the former academic dean of Spelman College; she is an associate professor of sociology and director of the United Negro College Fund/Andrew Mellon Programs.*

MANJU PARIKH *is an associate professor in the Department of Political Science at the College of Saint Benedict and Saint John's University; she has taught several courses dealing with gender issues and is currently researching global masculinities.*

4

This chapter identifies significant barriers to developing effective programs and services for men and offers a framework for addressing this growing problem.

Connecting Men to Academic and Student Affairs Programs and Services

Tracy Davis, Jason A. Laker

> The important fact of men's lives is not that they are biological males, but that they become men. Our sex may be male, but our identity as men is developed through a complex process of interaction with the culture in which we both learn the gender scripts appropriate to our culture and attempt to modify those scripts to make them more palatable.
> —Kimmel and Messner (1998, p. ix)

These words provide an insightful view of the developmental journey men undertake in search of a salient identity. This important reality, however, is often overlooked by educators and student affairs professionals. Even though we now understand that young women lose their voices and suffer many negative consequences largely associated with societal stereotypes about gender, educators have generally not made this connection in their practice with men. According to Pollack (1998), our insights about women's development have resulted "in helping girls gain greater freedom, speak in their true voices, be heard, and become empowered so they can better develop their individual capacities and strengths as women" (p. xxi). But what about our understanding of men's development and our success in promoting healthy growth?

There is significant evidence that our male students are struggling. The lack of engagement of college men in student and academic affairs programs and services is well documented in this volume (Kellom's Editor's Notes, and Clayton, Lucas Hewitt, and Gaffney's chapter). There is, moreover, a wealth of evidence that men on campus are in crisis. According to Capraro (2000), for example, "men outnumber women in virtually every category of drinking behavior used in research for comparison—prevalence, consumption, frequency of drinking and intoxication, incidence of heavy and problem drinking, alcohol abuse and dependence, and alcoholism" (p. 308). More often than not, the victims of violence in every category except sexual assault are men (Farrell, 1993). In addition, suicide is the third leading cause of death among males age fifteen to twenty-four; boys kill themselves at four times the rate of young women (National Center for Injury Prevention and Control, 1999).

Clearly these engagement, retention, and performance trends suggest that current strategies are not working. At the heart of the problem is a failure to accurately understand men's development. As Capraro powerfully argues earlier in this volume, we are generally at a loss to explain problems of the performance, persistence, and engagement of college men. It may be tempting to hold men themselves responsible for not connecting to our academic and student affairs programs and services, but we argue that it is a professional mandate to provide opportunities that incorporate an understanding of men's development. A look inward at our own student affairs profession offers insight into men's lack of engagement and how to address it.

In an effort to better understand why student affairs professionals are not more effectively engaging college men, we first identify professional socialization practices that contribute to the problem. We then offer a conceptual framework and suggest strategies for more effectively engaging and designing educational interventions for men. Finally, we identify and briefly describe several programs that are currently employing these concepts and strategies.

Barriers to Developing Effective Programs and Services for College Men

Student affairs professionals have an especially significant role to play in the retention and psychosocial development of all students. As in any field, student affairs has identified values, norms, and best practices that are inculcated into graduate students and new professionals. To better understand how practitioners make sense of and engage male students, we must examine the professional socialization process.

Professionals look to a variety of resources in order to do their work effectively, and they prioritize those resources according to perception of utility (Young and Coldwell, 1993). Professional practice is influenced by graduate preparation, workplace socialization, and personal attributes such as curiosity and temperament (Reio, 1997). Although formal research and theory exist relative to male identity development, such information is not generally included in graduate preparation programs (King, 1994) or in new staff training. Rather, issues related to women and people of color are discussed overtly, while men's issues are overlooked or seen as implied in discussion of general student developmental models. Even though college student personnel (CSP) programs include developmental theory based on research that sometimes uses only male subjects, such studies have not viewed their male subjects as gendered beings. Meth and Pasick (1990) argue that "although psychological writing has been androcentric, it has also been gender blind and it has assumed a male perspective but has not really explored what it means to be a man any more than what it means to be a woman" (p. vii). Thus, to integrate formal knowledge of male identity issues into professional practice, one must engage in self-directed pursuit. If the theoretical underpinnings of the profession neglect considerations of men's gender identity, the profession cannot adequately do one of its stated jobs, which is to facilitate students' identity development (ACPA, 1994; Barr and Keating, 1985; ACE, 1949).

A lack of understanding related to (or an assumption that we already understand) men's development leads to either reliance on stereotypical gender scripts or failure to consider men as gendered beings. Both are problematic and unprofessional. For example, student affairs professionals are taught to consider identity dimensions when working with women, people of color, openly gay people, and other students who possess an obvious target identity. Such consideration leads to better practice, because as one reflects on a student's identity one can interrupt hegemonic messages we've all learned and treat the individual in a more human and less "templatized" manner. Students are seen and heard as people whose experiences shape their behavior and interactions. In a disturbing irony, ignoring the salience of gender or race in white male students reifies the privilege of those agent groups to the extent that invisibility perpetuates privilege.

Lacking a conceptual framework and professional training, even effective engagement of men may be rooted in hegemonic assumptions (Nylund and Nylund, 2003). Thus the mechanisms designed to facilitate development are using barometers that perpetuate rather than challenge existing gender scripts. For programs and services to be effective in terms of promoting male students' identity development (or indeed to even be enticing to men so that they participate), they must draw upon theoretical and practical understanding of male identity. We now turn our attention to identification of a barometer, or theoretical framework, to assess the potential for a program or service to be effective with men.

A Framework for Designing Services for College Men

Developmental interventions with men need to be guided by three fundamental questions: Are they consistent with what we know about developmental theory and the socially constructed contours that shape men's development? Do they recognize important differences among men and masculinities? Do they balance challenge with support? Our answers to these questions determine, to a large extent, our success in effectively promoting men's growth and development.

Developmental Theory

There is an emerging conceptual base that can help us understand men's development (Davis, 2002; Brod and Kaufman, 1994; Kimmel and Messner, 2004; O'Neil, 1981, 1990; Pollack, 1998). It is first necessary to avoid being seduced into believing that past theories of human development already tell us what we need to know about men's development. Scher (1990), for example, cautions that men "must always be viewed in the context of the restraints, constraints, and expectations of the male gender role [because] men are inextricably entwined with the demands of our culture" (p. 325). In other words, if we are to understand college men we must understand the social construction of masculinity and the pressure for men to conform to these standards.

O'Neil (1981, 1990) offers a useful framework for understanding the conflict men experience resulting from the societal press to conform to traditional masculinity. The negative consequences associated with trying to conform to the traditional male role have been termed "gender-role conflict" (O'Neil and others, 1986). Gender-role conflict is defined as "a psychological state in which socialized gender roles have negative consequences on a person or others" (Stillson, O'Neil, and Owen, 1991, p. 458). O'Neil and others (1986) developed a gender role conflict scale comprising four factors that theoretically correspond to specific aspects of the male role: restrictive emotionality; socialized control, power, and competition; restrictive sexual and affectionate behavior; and obsession with achievement, work, and success.

Student affairs professionals need to understand these characteristics as part of the routine socialization men receive in American culture. The phrase "be a man," for example, serves to restrict men's full range of emotionality. Professionals can more effectively promote development by using theory to understand the possible genesis of behavior. If a man makes a homophobic statement, how would practitioners react differently if they see the comment as hateful ignorance, as opposed to a natural response to men's fear of femininity rooted in social taboos related to male affection? Do we respond to the behavior as a character flaw, or as an artifact of absorbing the gendered messages consistently reinforced in the culture? This is not to suggest that offensive or hurtful behavior should be tolerated. Rather, this framework contextualizes it such that a more purposeful and effective intervention can be devised by the practitioner.

Programs and other interventions can also be designed using the gender role conflict theoretical framework. For example, the first author of this chapter uses contemporary sitcoms and entertainment media to illustrate gender role conflict themes and challenges participants to (1) view messages they receive about being a man more critically and (2) make their own decisions, in spite of cultural pressure. Career development professionals can focus on men's obsession with achievement, work, and success; residence life staff can offer all-male sexual assault prevention programs consistent with socialized control and power; and Greek life professionals can open discussion with fraternity men about the impact of gender role conflict on how and which (and under what conditions) emotions are expressed and relationships developed.

Recent research on men clearly illustrates the value of gender role conflict theory in understanding and working with men (Davis, 2002; Davis and Liddell, 2002; Good and Wood, 1995). Restrictive emotionality and inexpressiveness has long been a barrier to working successfully with men. Fortunately, there is an emerging body of research that offers practical strategies for working more developmentally with men. Pollack (1998) discovered, for example, that "many mothers find that if they engage in action-oriented activities with their sons, their boys began to open up and talk" (p. 101). Instead of relying on the popular myth that men are simply inexpressive, student affairs professionals should consider how physical activity might be used to promote men's expression. At a recent workshop presented by one of the authors, a graduate student illustrated this point when she told about playing video games with the male resident assistants she supervises in order to communicate more effectively with them.

In specific terms, Pollack (2001) offers strategies for facilitating discussion with men:

- Create a safe space
- Give men time to feel comfortable with expression
- Seek out and provide alternative pathways for expression (that is, relate while engaging in action-oriented activities)
- Listen without judging
- Avoid shaming
- Give affirmation and affection

Student affairs professionals should consider engaging men in action-oriented activities such as going for a walk or some other "doing" activity in order to get beyond the mask of masculinity.

Developmental theory and subsequent research offer critical guidelines for designing learning interventions with college men. In addition to asking whether interventions are consistent with what our knowledge base says about men, student affairs professionals need to ask if programs and staff adequately recognize important differences among men.

Multiple Masculinities

Linear-stage models of development fail to capture the range of masculinities that exist, which results in the impression that all men develop in the same way. The practical result of such an impression is practitioners using a bag-of-tricks approach to fit all contexts and intervention strategies as if they work for all men. A model that more accurately portrays development and the resulting array of masculinities is the Jones and McEwen Multiple Dimensions of Identity (MDI) model (2000). In their model, sexual orientation, race, culture, class, religion, and gender are dimensions central to one's identity. The salience of a particular dimension to one's core identity depends on changing contexts, among them current experiences, family background, sociocultural conditions, career decisions, and life planning. This model offers a template for gauging both individual interventions with and institutional programs for college men.

As a practical tool for working with college men, student affairs professionals can use the MDI as a mental framework to avoid making assumptions about the individual men with whom they are working. This tool encourages professionals to consider how intersections of sexual orientation, race, culture, religion, and gender might affect a student. Rather than assuming, for example, that sexual orientation is a central aspect of one's identity or even making assumptions about a student's sexuality, practitioners are encouraged to consider the range of possibilities. Another example is the all-too-human tendency to assume that men are masculine-gendered. Spence and Helmreich (1978) have persuasively demonstrated that men can be feminine-gendered. How would such a possibility have an impact on our interactions with, for example, a 6'4" male football player whose gender identity is predominantly feminine?

In terms of a template for evaluating the institutional program offerings for men, the MDI can help gauge whose needs are being met and who may be marginalized. Planners should ask, Who makes up our campus community? What programs are being offered for men representing various identities? In addition to guidelines to assess the target and breadth of interventions with men, it is critical to evaluate the quality of such interventions.

Challenge and Support

Central to the quality of our learning strategies is a clear understanding of the balance between challenge and support. Davis (2002) found that college men felt a lack of support in their environment. In a patriarchal culture men are privileged, but this should not keep us from treating men developmentally. Pollack (1990) challenges us to "be sensitively aware [and less countertransferentially critical] of the particular forms of affiliative needs and capacities shown by men" (p. 318). Student affairs professionals need to be alert to any disposition to rely on sex role expectations in deciding on developmentally appropriate challenges and supports.

As mentioned earlier in this chapter, absent a conceptual basis for understanding how men develop, student affairs professionals may rely on hegemonic masculinity. Pollack (1998) illustrates this when he argues that too often "teachers, rather than exploring the emotional reasons behind a boy's misconduct, may instead apply behavioral control techniques that are intended somehow to better 'civilize' boys" (p. 17). Do our judicial hearings reflect an understanding of developmental issues related to men? Do our sanctions reflect gender bias? Brody's research (1996) further illustrates how the social construction of gender may influence developmental interventions with men. She found that mothers talk more about sadness or distress with daughters and more about anger with sons. One result is a minimization of boys' attempts to dwell on sadness. Boys learn early on that expression of sadness is responded to far less warmly than expression of injustice. A student affairs professional untrained in considering how the social construction of gender identity might affect intervention with male students might unintentionally reinforce what Pollack (1998) calls the gender role straitjacket.

Kegan (1982) offers a practical antidote to the ineffective "bad dog" (Laker, 2003) strategy. In a description of learner positions and corresponding facilitative environments, Kegan suggests that we should meet the psychological position of defending with confirmation, surrendering with contradiction, and reintegrating with continuity. Rather than challenging a student who has written homophobic graffiti on a residence hall poster, for example, with arguments about sexual orientation or exclusively punitive sanctions, student affairs professionals should meet this behavior with confirmation. According to Kegan, confirmation can take the form of identifying commonalities with the student; establishing and modeling ground rules for respectful listening; affirming that it's OK to be uninformed and confused; and identifying misinformation, stereotypes, or assumptions. Essentially, the homophobia that may be at the heart of the negative behavior is met with creation of a safe environment where defenses are more permeable. Understanding of men's identity development, which O'Neil (1981) and others claim is fundamentally rooted in fear of femininity, and awareness of societal messages that promote fear of intimacy among men, should help student affairs professionals further understand the need to meet homophobic statements first with a strategy of confirmation. Men feeling confirmed and understood are more likely to express emotions such as confusion and fear. Just as Helms (1992) suggests that we approach people struggling with racism as fearful children, student affairs professionals should consider that in spite of the socially constructed mask of masculinity worn by many of our male students, underneath there might be a fearful boy. Once confirmation is used, students are more likely to surrender dogmatic positions, paving the way for subsequent strategies related to contradiction and continuity (Kegan, 1982).

If we are to begin to effectively engage college men and address their needs, student affairs professionals must assess whether or not interventions (1) are grounded in theory and research about men, (2) recognize differences among men and masculinities, and (3) provide support in addition to challenge.

Case Examples of Services for College Men

There are a growing number of programs and services on college campuses that are rooted in a fundamental understanding of men's gender identity development. Some examples worthy of consideration as benchmarks are described here.

• Center for Men's Leadership and Service, Saint John's University, Minnesota (http://www.csbsju.edu/menscenter) Approved by the Board of Regents in 2002, the center has a mission of creating a safe and respectful environment for students to share their stories, explore the masculine condition in a holistic setting, conduct research, and do programming. Student research projects are under way on international men's stories, changing men's perceptions of masculinity, men's spirituality, and AIDS education. Programming includes an annual Men's Lives Series, annual conference on the college male, and outreach to the community. Students may participate by volunteering, taking a course, or arranging an internship. Presentations have been made at the American Men's Studies Association, NASPA, ACPA, and other regional conferences.

• Pierce College (Washington) men's programs and services (http://www.pierce.ctc.edu/mensprogram/) Pierce College, a public, two-year school with sixty-seven hundred students, has campuses in Puyallup and at Fort Steilacoom in Lakewood. The Men's Program is a both a center and a confederation of faculty and staff who offer educational programs, hold support groups for men, and conduct research about men's development. Staff also visit regional high schools and postsecondary institutions throughout the Puget Sound region to discuss the importance of understanding men's issues and how they have informed successes with students at Pierce.

There are several programs and services offered by the Men's Programs staff. The Men's Forum is an ongoing male student support group operating since 1995. The groups are leaderless and encourage open and respectful dialogue in a confidential setting. The Men's Mentorship Program, begun in 1999, is a more formal activity wherein mentors and mentees establish a written contract intended to explicitly outline how the relationship will operate to promote the mentee's success in college. The Men's Program also offers a lecture series on issues such as fathering, relationship violence, intimacy, and other topics related to men's development. In 2003, the Men's Program convened a conference on men and boys in education at the Puyallup campus.

• Dartmouth's Men's Project (http://www.dartmouth.edu/~cwg/mens.html) The Men's Project operates from the Center for Women and Gender at Dartmouth College in Hanover, New Hampshire. The program invites male students to participate in educational sessions and activities aimed at preventing sexual violence and promoting affirming development of men's identities. The program operates on the assumption that "all students value equity and safety, and [it seeks] to support male students' commitment to realizing these values, whether through individual actions or group activities."

The program offers public events with national and campus-based speakers on topics such as masculinity and violence, gender communication, and pornography, as well as conducting antisexism and antirape work. Weekly discussions, collaboration with fraternities and other student groups, training programs, and community events are offered through the program as well. In 2003, two hundred middle school boys and girls came to the Dartmouth campus for companion programs, Boys Speak Out, and Sister to Sister, which focused on the transition into adulthood by exploring issues of self-esteem, dating, communicating with peers, violence, and formation of mentoring relationships with college students.

Conclusion

The alarming statistics that suggest college men may be doing much worse than we might imagine should serve as a call to action for the student affairs profession. We consider the research and resources that new professionals are drawing upon for working developmentally with male students inadequate. Quite simply, student affairs professionals need to better understand college men within the contours of socially constructed identities. Our professional obligation to promote the healthy development of female and male students requires more focused attention on appropriate learning strategies. An understanding of men's development, the multiple dimensions of identity, and appropriate levels of challenge and support will help student affairs professionals more effectively connect men to academic and student services.

In a recent conversation with a female colleague, one of the authors heard real trepidation about the theoretical and philosophical framework described herein. The behavior of an agent population (for example, men) can have the effect of marginalizing target groups (women, people of color, gays and lesbians, and so on). To respond to a male student's hurtful behavior, a professional who represents one of the target identities must balance the need to be developmental with the internal sense of pain this behavior may trigger. This is not an easy prospect, but we believe that the developmental approach has a great likelihood of promoting positive change and reducing oppression, both individually and institutionally.

References

American College Personnel Association (ACPA). "The Student Learning Imperative: Implications for Student Affairs." Washington, D.C.: ACPA, 1994.
American Council on Education (ACE). "The Student Personnel Point of View" (rev. ed.). American Council on Education Studies Series 6, no. 13. Washington, D.C.: ACE, 1949.

Barr, M. J., Keating, L. A., and Associates (eds.). *Developing Effective Student Services Programs: Systematic Approaches for Practitioners.* San Francisco: Jossey-Bass, 1985.

Brod, H., and Kaufman, M. (eds.). *Theorizing Masculinities.* Thousand Oaks, Calif.: Sage, 1994.

Brody, L. R. "Gender, Emotional Expression, and the Family." In R. Kavanaugh, B. Zimmerberg-Glick, and S. Fein (eds.), *Emotion: Interdisciplinary Perspectives.* Hillsdale, N.J.: Erlbaum, 1996.

Capraro, R. L. "Why College Men Drink: Alcohol, Adventure, and the Paradox of Masculinity." *Journal of American College Health,* 2000, *48*(6), 307–315.

Davis, T. L. "Voices of Gender Role Conflict: The Social Construction of College Men's Identity." *Journal of College Student Development,* 2002, *43*(4), 508–521.

Davis, T. L., and Liddell, D. L. "Getting Inside the House: The Effectiveness of a Rape Prevention Program for College Fraternity Men." *Journal of College Student Development,* 2002, *43*(1), 35–50.

Farrell, W. *The Myth of Male Power.* New York: Simon and Schuster, 1993.

Good, G. E., and Wood, P. K. "Male Gender Role Conflict, Depression, and Help Seeking: Do College Men Face Double Jeopardy?" *Journal of Counseling and Development,* 1995, *74*(1), 70–75.

Helms, J. E. *A Race Is a Nice Thing to Have: A Guide to Being a White Person, or Understanding the White Persons in Your Life.* Topeka, Kans.: Content Communications, 1992.

Jones, S. R., and McEwen, M. K. "A Conceptual Model of Multiple Dimensions of Identity." *Journal of College Student Development,* 2000, *41*(4), 405–414.

Kegan, R. *The Evolving Self.* Cambridge, Mass.: Harvard University Press, 1982.

Kimmel, M., and Messner, M. (eds.). *Men's Lives* (4th ed.). Boston: Allyn and Bacon, 1998.

Kimmel, M., and Messner, M. (eds.). *Men's Lives* (6th ed.). Boston: Allyn and Bacon, 2004.

King, P. M. "Theories of College Student Development: Sequences and Consequences." *Journal of College Student Development,* 1994, *35*(6), 413–421.

Laker, J. "Bad Dogs: Rethinking Our Engagement of Male Students." In P. Brown (ed.), *Men On Campus Series.* Washington, D.C.: Standing Committee for Men, American College Personnel Association, 2003.

Meth, R. L., and Pasick, R. S. *Men in Therapy: The Challenge of Change.* New York: Guilford Press, 1990.

National Center for Injury Prevention and Control, Centers for Disease Prevention and Control. "Suicide Deaths and Rates per 100,000." 1999. http://www.cdc.gov/ncipc/data/us9794/Suic.html. Accessed April 23, 2004.

Nylund, D., and Nylund, D. "Narrative Therapy as Counter-Hegemonic Practice." *Men and Masculinities,* 2003, *5*(4), 386–394.

O'Neil, J. M. "Patterns of Gender Role Conflict and Strain: Sexism and Fear of Femininity in Men's Lives." *Personnel and Guidance Journal,* 1981, *60,* 203–210.

O'Neil, J. M. "Assessing Men's Gender Role Conflict." In D. Moore and F. Leafgren (eds.), *Problem-Solving Strategies and Interventions for Men in Conflict.* Alexandria, Va.: American Counseling Association, 1990.

O'Neil, J. M., and others. "Gender Role Conflict Scale: College Men's Fear of Femininity." *Sex Roles,* 1986, *14*(5–6), 335–350.

Pollack, W. S. "Men's Development and Psychotherapy: A Psychoanalytic Perspective." *Psychotherapy,* 1990, *27,* 316–321.

Pollack, W. S. *Real Boys: Rescuing Our Sons from the Myths of Boyhood.* New York: Holt, 1998.

Pollack, W. S. *Real Boys Workbook: The Definitive Guide to Understanding and Interacting with Boys of All Ages.* New York: Villard, 2001.

Reio, T. G. "Effects of Curiosity on Socialization-Related Learning and Job Performance in Adults." Unpublished doctoral dissertation, Virginia Polytechnic Institute and State University, *Dissertation Abstracts International*, 58/9-A, 3393, 1997.

Scher, M. "Effect of Gender Role Incongruities on Men's Experience as Clients in Psychotherapy." *Psychotherapy*, 1990, 27, 322–326.

Spence, J. T., and Helmreich, R. *Masculinity and Femininity: Their Psychological Dimensions, Correlates, Antecedents.* Austin: University of Texas Press, 1978.

Stillson, R., O'Neil, J., and Owen, S. "Predictors of Adult Men's Gender Role Conflict: Race, Class, Unemployment, Age, Instrumentality-Expressiveness, and Personal Strain." *Journal of Counseling Psychology*, 1991, 38(4), 458–464.

Young, R., and Coldwell, L. "Perceptions of the Utility of Professional Education Topics." *Journal of College Student Development*, 1993, 34(6), 63–68.

TRACY DAVIS is an associate professor of college student personnel and program coordinator in the Educational and Interdisciplinary Studies Department at Western Illinois University.

JASON A. LAKER is the dean of campus life at Saint John's University in Collegeville, Minnesota, and an adjunct faculty member in the honors and women's studies programs at Saint Cloud State University.

A sobering description of the state of college men's health is followed by discussion of the Six-Point HEALTH Plan and strategies for educational campaigns, marketing, and outreach efforts.

Best Practices for Improving College Men's Health

Will H. Courtenay

The greatest gender gap in mortality occurs among fifteen-to-twenty-four-year-olds (DHHS, 2000). Three out of every four deaths annually in this age group are male. The death rate is highest for African American men, followed by Hispanic and European American men. Although disease, injury, and death rates are unavailable for college students specifically, a general profile of college men's health can be inferred from the risks of this approximate age group. Among adolescents, males are more likely than females to be hospitalized for injuries. Fatal injuries account for more than 80 percent of all deaths among fifteen-to-twenty-four-year-old men, and three out of four injury deaths in this age group are male. Young men of this age are also at far greater risk than women for sexually transmitted diseases or infections (STDs/STIs). Despite these risks, the gender-specific health care needs of college men have only recently begun to be examined (Courtenay, 1998, 1999; Courtenay and Keeling, 2000a, 2000b).

Explaining College Men's Poor Health

The gender gap in longevity is explained largely by men's health behaviors and beliefs—including beliefs about manhood.

Beliefs and Behaviors. Biological factors are relatively poor predictors of gender differences in disease and death, which are explained largely by men's health beliefs and behaviors (Courtenay, 2003). For example, men are less likely than women to believe that personal behaviors contribute to good health or to accept personal responsibility for their health (Courtenay,

2001a, 2003). Similarly, men respond to stress in less healthy ways than women do. They are less likely than women to employ healthy, vigilant coping strategies and more likely to use avoidant coping strategies such as denial, distraction, and increased alcohol consumption (Stanton and Courtenay, 2003).

Men are also more likely than women to engage in more than thirty behaviors that are associated with an increased risk of disease, injury, and death (Courtenay, 2000a). Among college students specifically, men engage in fewer health-promoting behaviors than women—including wearing safety belts; eating well; conducting self-examinations for cancer; and behaviors related to driving, sleep, and exercise (Courtenay, 1998, 2000a). College men also engage in more risky behaviors than college women do, among them behaviors related to sex, drug use, carrying weapons, and physically fighting; and they take greater risks while playing sports and driving.

Compared to college women, college men are more likely to drink alcohol, to drink more of it, and to drink more often—as well as drive under the influence of alcohol. Consequently, college men experience more negative health consequences of drinking, notably physical injury, infection from STDs/STIs and HIV, drowning, and motor vehicle death. College men are also more likely to use tobacco and have more dangerous smoking habits such as smoking more cigarettes per day (Courtenay, 1998, 2000a). Consumption of smokeless tobacco has increased among young men between 250 and 300 percent since the 1970s and is typically initiated during college. These gender differences in health beliefs and behaviors remain among college students across various ethnic groups (Courtenay, McCreary, and Merighi, 2002).

Masculinity. Although simply being male is linked with poor health behavior and increased health risks, so is gender, or men's beliefs about "being a man." Men who adopt traditional attitudes about manhood have greater health risks than men with less traditional attitudes. Among college students, traditional attitudes have been linked with a higher level of anxiety, greater cardiovascular reactions to stress, maladaptive coping, depression, and poor health behaviors related to smoking, alcohol and drug use, safety, diet, sleep, and sexual practices. Furthermore, these men are more likely than nontraditional men not to seek help from others and underuse professional services on campus. African American men are more likely than men of other ethnic groups to endorse traditional attitudes about masculinity (Courtenay, 2000b, 2001b, 2002).

How College Men Learn Unhealthy Beliefs and Behaviors

There is high agreement in U.S. society about what are considered to be typical feminine and masculine characteristics (see Courtenay, 2000c). It is not surprising, then, that people treat girls and boys differently. In fact, regardless of gender, people interact with an infant on the basis of what they believe to be the infant's gender. Similarly, clear distinctions are drawn in the media between men's and women's behaviors—including men's and women's health behaviors. These lessons can last a lifetime.

Peers, Parents, and Other Adults. From birth, parents treat girls and boys differently (Courtenay, 2000c). Despite the fact that boys are at relatively greater risk, parents are less concerned about the safety of their sons than they are about the safety of their daughters. Boys are handled more roughly, are engaged in more intense and competitive play, are physically punished more, and are exposed to more violence. Boys are also more likely than girls to be discouraged from seeking help, and to be punished when they do seek help. This differential treatment has both short-term and long-term effects on the health of men and boys (Courtenay, 2000b, 2000c).

It is not only parents but peers and other adults who teach boys unhealthy beliefs and behaviors (Courtenay, 2000b, 2000c, 2003). North Americans strongly endorse the cultural (and health-related) beliefs or stereotypes that men are independent, self-reliant, strong, robust, and tough. When people are told that an infant is male regardless of its actual gender, they are more likely to believe that it is "firmer" and "less fragile" than when they are told that the same infant is female. Men and boys experience comparatively greater social pressure than women and girls to endorse traditional beliefs about gender.

Media. On television and in films, men are shown smoking three to seven times more often than women. Two-thirds of all characters who drink in prime-time television programs are men. In general, women and girls are portrayed in the media as having the greatest health risks and being the most likely to die, while men and boys are portrayed as engaging in unhealthy or high-risk behaviors—and as being healthy and invulnerable to the risks that their high-risk behaviors pose.

Alcohol and tobacco advertisements are strategically placed in magazines and television programs with predominantly male audiences. For example, *Sports Illustrated,* the magazine most often read by college men, has more tobacco and alcohol advertisements than any other. Advertisers also often portray men in high-risk activities to sell their products. Beer commercials, for example, have been found to link men's drinking with taking risks and facing danger without fear. Tobacco companies link the use of smokeless tobacco with virility and athletic performance in marketing to men. These media representations of gender and health have been found to contribute to negative health effects for men and boys (Courtenay, 2000c).

Conflicting Messages About Manhood and Health. College men receive contradictory (and consequently confusing) messages about health (Courtenay, 1998, 2000c). Even though health education campaigns attempt to teach young men that it is wrong to be violent, on television men and boys are more likely than women and girls to initiate and engage in physically violent behavior, which typically is rewarded and without negative consequences (see Courtenay, 2000c). Not surprisingly, nearly one in seven college men in California gets into a physical fight in one year (Patrick and others, 1997). Health messages encouraging abstinence and tobacco cessation similarly contradict consistent messages young men receive from the media, and society in general, indicating that both drinking and tobacco use are simply part of being a man (Courtenay, 2000c). Given this, it is not surprising that college men use more alcohol and tobacco than college women.

Evidence-Based Strategies for College Health Professionals: The Six-Point HEALTH Plan

Research indicates that students often need gender-specific interventions, such as safer-sex education specifically tailored for women and men (Courtenay, 1998). I have developed a clinical practice guideline for health professionals who work with men (Courtenay, 2001a; Stanton and Courtenay, 2003), which is summarized here. Its recommendations are based on an extensive review of research. This Six-Point HEALTH Plan identifies behavioral and psychosocial factors that affect the onset, progression, and management of men's health problems; reviews evidence demonstrating the effectiveness of various interventions; and outlines specific best practices for addressing these factors when working with college men. Whether a health professional is treating college men in a health service, developing gender-specific programming for men, conducting outreach, or designing health education materials, the same basic principles of the Six-Point Plan hold true.

Any contact a health professional has with a college man represents an important opportunity. In general, men (including college men) are less likely than women to seek health care (Courtenay, 1998, 2000b). Therefore any encounter a health professional has with a college man may be the *only* opportunity for assessment and intervention that *any* health professional will have with that man for a long time. Furthermore, even one contact with a male patient can have significantly positive effects on both behavioral and clinical outcomes (Courtenay, 2001a).

The practice guideline addresses communication between clinicians and their patients, which is associated with treatment compliance and patient health status (see Courtenay, 2001a). College health professionals whose responsibility it is to counsel men in any capacity are in a unique position to assist these men. Research indicates that people are more likely to be helped to prevent future disease by health professionals who ask, educate, and counsel them about personal health behaviors than by those who perform physical examinations or tests (Courtenay, 2001a).

Each of the six subsections here briefly summarizes one of six types of intervention discussed in the clinical practice guideline. Together, the titles of the six points form an acronym that spells HEALTH: Humanize, Educate, Assume the worst, Locate supports, Tailor a plan, and Highlight strengths.

Humanize. Humanizing is a technique that validates or normalizes patients' health problems and concerns. Conveying to patients that their feelings and experiences are understandable or legitimate—and that other people would probably feel the same way—is considered essential to effective communication with patients (Courtenay, 2001a). Because disease, disability, and health-promoting responses to illness are antithetical to masculinity, men can experience embarrassment and shame when they do have health problems that they must address (Courtenay, 2001a). Clinicians can compensate for this and help men learn that asking for help, acknowledging pain, expressing fear, crying, or needing bed rest are normal, human experiences; they are not unmanly. Moderate self-disclosure on a clinician's part, particularly if the clinician is a man, may make a male patient feel safer and is associated with positive outcomes. You might say, "I know what you mean; I have a hard time admitting when I'm sick too."

Humanize Help Seeking. Men have less intention to seek help from a variety of sources when they need it (Courtenay, 2001a). Seeking help can undermine a man's sense of independence and be experienced as demeaning, which may lead to feelings of inadequacy and shame. Reconceptualize a student's help seeking as positive behavior, and offer reinforcement by saying, "Coming to see me when you did was the best thing you could have done." Reframing a man's seeking help as an act of strength, courage, and self-determination may decrease any embarrassment or self-doubt that he may experience in reaching out for help.

Humanize Illness and Convalescence. Because illness threatens masculine ideals of competence, vitality, and strength, men may experience illness as a personal flaw or a failure to successfully demonstrate manhood (Courtenay, 2000c). Simply saying, "You know, everybody gets sick sometimes" can bring relief to a man and help to establish rapport. When they are ill, men are less likely than women to restrict activities or stay in bed for both acute and chronic conditions (Courtenay, 2001a). Some men consider staying in bed to recover to be unnecessary "pampering." A college man may think of himself as "lazy" if he misses school or sports practice after an injury or operation. Humanize the need for convalescence by saying to a student, "Staying in bed and taking care of yourself when you're sick doesn't mean you're a not a team player."

Humanize Pain and Fear. Admitting or displaying fear and pain is largely unacceptable for men in our society. Not surprisingly, compared to women men report less pain for the same pathology, less severe pain, greater tolerance of pain, and a higher pain threshold. Although hormones may play some role in mediating the experience of pain, it is clear that psychosocial factors do too. Men report less pain to female clinicians than to male clinicians (Courtenay, 2003). The reluctance to acknowledge or report physical or emotional distress can have far-reaching implications for college men's health; it can influence help-seeking decisions, delay intervention, and undermine diagnosis and treatment planning.

In humanizing pain, health professionals should label conditions known to be painful as such: "Kidney stones can be very painful. I don't want you to hesitate for a moment if you think you might need to come back to get urgent care." Express surprise when a student denies that his kidney stones are painful. To more accurately assess a college man's level of pain, and to compensate for his potential minimization of pain, say, "There are no medals for enduring pain, so I want you to let me know if you experience even the *slightest* bit of discomfort."

Humanize Sexual Concerns. At least one out of four American men is unable to get or maintain an erection for sex, and almost all men—including college men—experience occasional and transient erectile problems. Erectile dysfunction is also a common side effect of a variety of medications (Courtenay, 2001a). These facts are inconsistent with the stereotype that men are perpetually interested in and ready for sex. Consequently, sexual dysfunction can threaten a student's self-image as a man, and it can be threatening to acknowledge it. Three out of four men with sexual concerns report being too embarrassed to discuss those concerns with their physician. To humanize college men's sexual concerns, problems, and fears say, "Most men have concerns about sex; it's normal. And I'd be surprised if you didn't." Help men identify unrealistic perceptions of manhood that contribute to sexual anxiety, and learn how human perceptions of sexuality can reduce stress and sexual dysfunction. You can say, "You're not a machine. Your body can't be expected to turn on and off at will."

Humanize Men's Body Image. Superhuman perceptions of manhood distort college men's perceptions of their bodies. Over the last several decades, cultural standards of the ideal male body have grown increasingly large and bulky. Not surprisingly, men and boys have become increasingly dissatisfied with their bodies. Research indicates that 28–68 percent of normal-weight young men either try to or want to gain weight, and that the desire to be bigger and more muscular is linked with traditional masculinity (Courtenay, 2003; McCreary, Saucier, and Courtenay, forthcoming). This desire in young men is also associated with psychological distress, impaired social functioning, and substance abuse, including abuse of anabolic steroids. College health professionals can teach this to college men and help them make human their superhuman perceptions of the male body.

Educate. Health education interventions are an essential aspect of disease and injury prevention and can reduce risks, improve compliance, facilitate change, and promote health (Courtenay, 2001a). Furthermore, research consistently indicates that men, including college men, are less knowledgeable than women about health in general, and about specific diseases (Courtenay, 1998, 2003). College men, for example, know significantly less than college women about self-examinations for cancer and risk factors for HIV.

Despite these findings, health professionals often fail to provide health education to men. For example, men are provided with fewer and briefer explanations—as well as less information overall—from clinicians during medical examinations (Roter and Hall, 1997). Only 29 percent of physicians routinely provide age-appropriate instruction on performing testicular self-examination (TSE), compared to 86 percent providing age-appropriate instruction to women on performing breast self-examination. Additionally, although men engage in more unhealthy behaviors, they are less likely than women to be counseled by clinicians about changing those behaviors. For example, college men are less likely than college women to be questioned in medical visits about tobacco use.

Specific educational interventions vary depending on a college man's current health, his presenting concern, and his future risks. A good way to start educating men is by communicating that "Most of the things that have the biggest impact on your health are completely within your control." When educating college men, it is essential to include even quite basic knowledge (such as whom to call for an appointment) because many men have had relatively little experience with health care. Educators should keep the information simple, offer written materials, and make statements and written materials both clear and direct. They should also provide alternative responses to unhealthy behaviors. It is also important to encourage questions, because men ask clinicians fewer questions than women do (Courtenay, 2001a). You can say, "I've explained a lot to you. I'd be surprised if you didn't have some questions."

College men also need to be taught the importance of early detection of disease. Screening tests and self-examinations are essential for preventing disease and identifying a variety of diseases at an early stage, which is when successful treatment is more likely (Courtenay, 2001a). However, men in general and African American men in particular are less likely than women to practice self-examination or to attend health screenings (Courtenay, 2001b, 2003). Self-examinations particularly relevant to college men include those for skin and testicular cancer, and STDs/STIs.

Assume the Worst. One of the most common and enduring cultural stereotypes about men is that they are healthier and more resistant to disease or injury than women, despite a wealth of evidence to the contrary (Courtenay, 2000c). Men who conform to these cultural stereotypes increase their health risks. They may try to appear strong and healthy, believe that they are invulnerable to risk, minimize pain and deny feelings that others may perceive as signs of weakness, and report their health inaccurately.

Among college students, men perceive less risk than women for a variety of health threats, among them risks associated with the use of cigarettes, alcohol, and other drugs; sun exposure; physically dangerous sports; and driving. For example, college men perceive less risk associated with not using a safety belt, drinking and driving, and not making a full stop at a stop sign. These beliefs are inconsistent with the finding that (in California, for example) men are at fault in nearly eight of ten automobile accidents and two of three injury crashes (Courtenay, 2000a); and among fifteen-to-twenty-four-year-olds twenty times more men than women die in automobile accidents, which are the leading cause of death in this age group (DHHS, 2000). Furthermore, college men's perceived invulnerability prevents them from changing unhealthy behaviors (Courtenay 1998, 2003).

The desire to conceal vulnerability can influence college men's decision not to seek care and can affect assessment and diagnosis when they do get care. Compared to college women, men are less likely to confide in friends, express vulnerability, disclose their problems, or seek help or support from others when they need it (Courtenay 1998a, 2000b, 2000c). Among college students with depression, for example, men are more likely than women to rely on themselves, withdraw socially, or try to talk themselves out of it (Courtenay, 2000c). These behavioral responses to depression contribute to explaining why young men represent six of seven deaths from suicide, which is the third leading cause of death in this age group (DHHS, 2000).

Taken together, these findings about men suggest that clinicians should assume the worst. An additional reason for assuming the worst is that health professionals can also be blinded by gender stereotypes and fooled by men's displays of invulnerability. Mental health clinicians, for example, are less likely to diagnose depression correctly in men than in women, which contributes to men's high suicide rate (Courtenay, 2003). Making matters worse, because of delays in their help seeking men's physical and mental conditions are often serious when they finally do seek help.

To diagnose a man's condition correctly and to plan his treatment, it is essential to elicit accurate information about his symptoms and emotional states. Asking a man, "How do you feel?" is not recommended. This question can be difficult for men to respond to, and it often elicits nothing more than a shrug of the shoulders or an unreflective "Fine." Instead, a health professional should inquire indirectly: "Tell me, how do you experience that?" Or, "What is that like for you?" These questions are uncommon and may be less likely to prompt an automatic response. In response to perceptions of vulnerability that are inconsistent with a man's actual risks, a clinician can say, "I know it's important to you to think of yourself as strong and healthy. But that attitude can lead you to take unnecessary risks with your health."

Locate Supports. Men are taught to value independence, autonomy, and self-sufficiency in themselves (Courtenay, 2000b). It is not surprising then that men (including college men) have fewer friendships and smaller social networks than women do, and that they tend not to use the support they do have. There is strong evidence that a lack of social support constitutes a risk factor for mortality, especially for men. Men with the lowest level of social support are much more likely to die than men with the highest level. In contrast, men with a higher level of social support maintain more positive health practices (Courtenay, 2000a).

It is essential for college health professionals to help men identify the sources of support that are available to them: significant others, friends, family, coworkers, classmates, and so forth. You can ask, "Who are the people you're most comfortable asking to give you a hand?" It is important then to encourage men to reach out to these people, because often they will not do so of their own accord. Health professionals can also help college men identify support or educational groups and social activities—such as church and organized sports—that can be valuable sources of social support. In talking with college men about social support, use concepts that are familiar to many men, such as teamwork and strategic planning. Suggest that the student set regular times to meet with friends. The routine ball game, movie, or dinner out gives a college man regular contact and support without his having to ask for it or betray his need for it.

Tailor a Plan. Tailoring a plan means devising a health maintenance plan (like a maintenance schedule for a car). A man is more likely to have a maintenance plan for his car than for himself. Developing and implementing such a plan is associated with improved treatment follow-through and behavioral change (Courtenay, 2001a). The type of plan, the extent of the plan, and its specific components depend on each man's individual needs, as well as on the clinician's role and functions. Ideally, a man's comprehensive health maintenance plan includes periodic physicals, screenings, self-examinations, preventive behaviors, self-care techniques, and vitamin and medicine schedules.

Tailoring the plan means individualizing it to the student's needs, age, intellectual capacity, attitudes, cultural background, and circumstances; this is considered essential both in establishing a plan and in fostering adherence. For the plan to be successful it must be realistic, it must be broken down into attainable steps, and the patient must have the skills necessary to carry it out. College health professionals should also invite the student's own input and suggestions, as well as help him identify potential obstacles. He may know, for example, that if he drinks he is not likely to use a condom. It is also beneficial to develop a verbal or written contract, with dates for achieving specific goals. All of these factors are associated with improved outcomes (Courtenay, 2001a).

Highlight Strengths. Highlighting a patient's strengths fosters motivation and compliance. It also conveys respect for his efforts and achievements, which is an important aspect of effective patient-clinician communication (Courtenay, 2001a). Although endorsement of traditional masculinity in general is associated with increased health risks among men, there are certain masculine-identified characteristics that are highly adaptive for men (and women). Among them are having the ability to act independently, be assertive, and be decisive (Courtenay, 2001a, 2003). Reliance on some specific masculine characteristics such as these has been found to help enable men to cope with cancer and chronic illness. Some specific strengths that should be highlighted are intellectualized and goal-oriented coping, a need for control, and a teamwork approach.

Begin by commenting on a student's strength before exploring his physical symptoms or emotional states. An example is to say, "It's great that you took control of things the way you did and got yourself in here so quickly." Because being intellectual, logical, and rational are highly valued coping mechanisms among men (Courtenay, 2001), health professionals should emphasize the intellectual aspects of health education. Similarly, men engage in more action-oriented, problem-solving, and goal-setting coping than women do (Courtenay, 2001). Goal setting is also an effective way to modify behavior and improve health (Courtenay, 2001a), so college health professionals can frame health goals as targets to shoot for. Similarly, they can capitalize on a student's talent for keeping baseball scores when he is tracking cholesterol, blood pressure, or behavioral change.

To maintain healthy behaviors and modify unhealthy ones, it is essential that people have a sense of self-efficacy or control, and to believe that they can respond effectively to reduce a health threat. College men who have a personal sense of control over cancer, for example, are more likely to practice monthly TSE (Courtenay, 2001b). Illness, however, can threaten a man's sense of being in control. Additionally, men are more likely than women to believe they have little or no control over their future health (Courtenay, 1998b, 2003). College health professionals can foster a student's sense of self-efficacy by focusing on the positive aspects of control, and suggesting that he take "personal responsibility" for his well-being and "take charge" of his health.

Emphasize teamwork too. For most men, health care is something that is done *to* them; it is not something in which they see themselves as active participants. Clinicians need to invite a man's active involvement and emphasize teamwork, which can be ideal for a man; men are often most comfortable engaging in relationships through action and by doing things, such as projects, together. This kind of patient-clinician collaboration is associated with positive health outcomes (Courtenay, 2001a). Asking "Where do you want to start?" enlists a man's involvement and reinforces his active participation.

Evidence-Based Strategies for Educational Campaigns, Marketing, and Outreach

The Six-Point Plan can also be applied to educational campaigns and marketing to college men. For example, these interventions can humanize by addressing the contradiction between human health care needs and masculinity, and assume the worst by addressing college men's perceived invulnerability to risk. Additional evidence-based strategies should guide the development of gender-specific educational campaigns, marketing, and outreach to men, which I discuss briefly next.

One example is research related to TSE educational brochures provided at many colleges. These brochures typically diagram how to conduct a testicular self-examination. On the basis of prior success educating women with materials diagramming breast self-examinations, we might expect TSE brochures to be similarly effective. According to emerging research, TSE instruction in general is indeed effective. College men also prefer written materials, such as brochures, over video instruction; they also prefer brief, specific checklists on how to perform TSE rather than more detailed instructions. Most important, according to one study college men prefer written materials with *no* diagrams of the male anatomy. These materials were also the most effective in promoting TSE (Morman, 2002).

As the preceding example illustrates, health education, marketing, and outreach efforts must take gender-based research into account if they are to be successful; what is effective with women is not necessarily effective with men. Stages-of-change research is another example of this.

The stages-of-change, or transtheoretical, model identifies five stages of change that people move through in modifying their behavior. The stages are precontemplation, contemplation, preparation, action, and maintenance (Prochaska, Norcross, and DiClemente, 1994). Precontemplators typically deny their problems or unhealthy behaviors. Contemplators recognize their problems and begin to seriously think about solving them. Extensive research generally indicates that women are more likely than men to be contemplating changing unhealthy behavior or already maintaining healthy habits (Courtenay, 2003).

The transtheoretical model has also identified interventions that are effective in helping people adopt healthier behavior at each stage. What women contemplators need most is assistance in identifying the causes and consequences of their behaviors, help in considering the pros and cons of changing, and support in maintaining their healthy lifestyles. What men precontemplators need most is increased awareness of their problems and education to help them begin to consider change. These strategies can be applied to interventions with individuals, and to educational, marketing, and outreach interventions. In fact, interventions that neglect to apply stage-specific strategies, or neglect to take people's readiness to change into account, are likely to fail.

According to this model, public health campaigns are often unsuccessful because they are typically designed for the small minority of people who are ready to change unhealthy behavior. However, people who are not ready to change (people who are more likely to be men) actively resist these campaigns. Precontemplators in particular are the hardest people to reach, because they typically deny that they have a problem. Health campaigns for men not ready to change—the men at greatest risk—are more likely to be effective when they are designed for precontemplators. For example, one newspaper ad for a smoking cessation self-help program was directed to "smokers who do not wish to change." This unusually worded advertisement drew four hundred precontemplators, which the researchers considered a great success (Prochaska, Norcross, and DiClemente, 1994). Interventions like this that effectively help men to simply *begin* contemplating the possibility of changing unhealthy behavior (which is the primary objective with precontemplators) actually double the probability that these men will ultimately change.

Another research-based approach that can be applied to gender-specific interventions with men is social norms marketing. According to social norms theory, unhealthy (and healthy) behavior is fostered by perceptions (often incorrect) of how one's peers behave (Berkowitz, 2003). For example, a college man might overestimate his peers' involvement in risky behavior, which would foster his own involvement in unhealthy behavior. Alternatively, he might underestimate his peers' adoption of healthy habits, which would discourage him from adopting healthy behavior. Social norms theory focuses on peers because they have been found to have the greatest influence in shaping individual behavior.

One common intervention based on this theory is a social norms marketing campaign, which promotes accurate, healthy norms. Research indicates that when college students' "perceived norm" is challenged with evidence of the "actual norm," the unhealthy behavior—such as heavy drinking—often decreases. Social norms marketing campaigns hold promise for addressing a variety of health concerns relevant to men. They can be used, for example, to change incorrect perceptions about men's indifference to health matters.

More than five hundred men at a small midwestern liberal arts college were recently surveyed. Results of this survey indicated that these men misperceived that most other male students (55 percent) were either not at all concerned or only a little concerned about their health as men. Actually, only 35 percent of students were unconcerned; most (65 percent) reported being either somewhat or very concerned about their health as men (unpublished data). On the basis of these data, a social norms marketing campaign could be designed to promote the true norm that men on this campus *are* interested in their health as men. Although it has yet to be developed, we can hypothesize, from prior research, that interest in and concern about men's health would increase among men on this campus if such a campaign were implemented.

Unfortunately, social marketing campaigns do not always work (Keeling, 2000). For example, students sometimes *underestimate,* rather than overestimate, their peers' unhealthy behavior. Social marketing is particularly ineffective with specific groups within a larger campus—groups such as fraternity men, for whom norms are riskier than they are for other groups on campus. It has been argued recently that new, alternative intervention methods are needed for these high-risk men (Carter and Kahnweiler, 2000). One new, innovative, evidence-based approach is based on "sensation seeking" research.

Sensation seekers are disinhibited people who seek thrills and adventure, lust for new experiences, and are easily bored (Zuckerman, 1994). The instrument measuring this trait determines whether a person is a high or low sensation seeker. Thirty years of research consistently indicates that men are more likely than women to be high sensation seekers. It also shows that high sensation seekers are more likely than low sensation seekers to engage in a variety of risky behaviors such as heavy alcohol use, drug use, cigarette smoking, dangerous driving, high-risk sexual activity, high-risk sports, and criminal activity. For example, adolescent high sensation seekers are twice as likely as low sensation seekers to report using beer and liquor, and two to seven times more likely to report drug use.

Recently, researchers at the University of Kentucky began studying intervention strategies based on these findings (Harrington and others, 2003). They hypothesized that because people who engage in unhealthy, high-risk behavior are more likely to be high sensation seekers who seek novel and stimulating experiences, health campaigns targeting this population would also need to be novel and stimulating. Findings from a growing body of research indicate that high sensation seekers do in fact prefer media and health campaigns that are novel, creative, or unusual. Additionally, campaigns are most effective when they are intense, exciting, and stimulating; are graphic and explicit; are complex and unconventional; are fast-paced; are suspenseful and dramatic; use close-ups; and have strong audio and visual effects. Although not all of these features need be included in a single message, the most effective messages have multiple features from this list. Research shows that high sensation seekers pay greater attention to antidrug public service announcements (PSAs) that incorporate these features than to PSAs that do not; they are also more likely to recall PSA content, phone a drug hotline, report a more negative attitude toward drug use, and report less intention to use. (Interestingly, high sensation seekers also prefer messages that do not preach, which is consistent with the transtheoretical model; preaching to, or nagging, a precontemplator about changing will actually make him more *resistant* to change.)

These findings are relevant to college health professionals (particularly those concerned about men's health) because sensation seekers are primarily men and because they include those students who engage in the riskiest behaviors. These are the men who, historically, have been the most difficult to reach and for whom traditional health campaigns are ineffective. Sensation-seeking intervention strategies can be applied to college radio PSAs and to flyers and posters. They can also be adopted when marketing to and conducting health fairs for men, which should be designed differently than health fairs for women. Another application of this evidence is to provide safe, high sensation seeking alternatives to risky activities. For example, at an all-male, liberal arts college in the Midwest a climbing wall was set up and made available on the most popular midweek drinking night. Although the effectiveness of this specific intervention has yet to be tested empirically, research suggests that this high sensation seeking alternative would effectively reduce drinking on this campus. The overwhelmingly enthusiastic response from students certainly suggests that it has been effective.

Conclusion

This chapter has presented an overview of psychosocial and behavioral factors that influence men's health and identified evidence-based strategies for addressing these factors. If college health professionals adopt these best practices, research indicates that college men will live longer, healthier lives. The final section lists some additional interventions for promoting health and well-being among college men. Although these strategies may prove helpful, future research is needed to determine whether they are actually effective, and if so, with which men; and whether they are more effective with college men than with college women.

Health Promotion Strategies for College Men

- Offer convenient and free or low-cost services, such as screenings and immunizations.
- Provide a confidential telephone health line.
- Bring services and education to men (classes, sports events, fraternities, and fitness centers).
- Furnish incentives (such as free promotional items, food, tickets to sports events, academic credit for attendance, or requiring attendance).
- Offer free men's health kits or fanny packs with educational materials such as self-examination instructions and health service information, along with promotional items, such as healthy protein bars and toiletries.
- Develop a health mentoring project with upperclassmen educating lowerclassmen.
- Address the needs of special populations of men (for example, gay and bisexual men, men of color).
- Identify students who have experienced health problems (testicular cancer, auto accidents) as spokesmen and peer health educators.
- Use high-profile spokesmen to promote men's health through media campaigns or for special events (community leaders, athletes, actors or media personalities).
- Offer competitive contests with prizes for involvement in health promotion activities.
- Attach men's health education information to prescriptions.
- Develop health events with a theme (for instance, related to pop culture, rock music, or sports).
- Make available health promotion and education to men in urgent care.
- Use concepts that appeal to men (like "health coaching" and "teamwork") in marketing and education materials.
- Make use of men's bathrooms and locker rooms for distribution of health education materials and for health campaigns.
- Provide e-mail-based education and Internet survey tools or games.

- Offer a "sports and fitness expo" with health and wellness components, as well as sports events, competitions, sporting equipment, and exhibitions.
- Design activities around National Men's Health Week (the week including and ending on Father's Day), featuring lectures, forums, debates, media campaigns, displays, workshops, and presentations.
- Hire male staff and clinicians and make them available to men.
- Create opportunities for men to talk about health issues in small discussion groups (for example, after peer educators speak to larger groups).
- Require entering freshmen to attend a workshop that addresses the health effects of masculinity and includes healthy strategies for adjusting to college life.

References

Berkowitz, A. D. "Applications of Social Norms Theory to Other Health and Social Justice Issues." In H. W. Perkins (ed.), *The Social Norms Approach to Preventing School and College-Age Substance Abuse.* San Francisco: Jossey-Bass, 2003.

Carter, C. A., and Kahnweiler, W. M. "The Efficacy of the Social Norms Approach to Substance Abuse Prevention Applied to Fraternity Men." *Journal of American College Health,* 2000, *49*(2), 66–70.

Courtenay, W. H. "College Men's Health: An Overview and a Call to Action." *Journal of American College Health,* 1998, *46*(6), 279–290.

Courtenay, W. H. "Youth Violence? Let's Call It What It Is." *Journal of American College Health,* 1999, *48*(3), 141–142.

Courtenay, W. H. "Behavioral Factors Associated with Disease, Injury, and Death Among Men: Evidence and Implications for Prevention." *Journal of Men's Studies,* 2000a, *9*(1), 81–142.

Courtenay, W. H. "Constructions of Masculinity and Their Influence on Men's Well-Being: A Theory of Gender and Health." *Social Science and Medicine,* 2000b, *50*(10), 1385–1401.

Courtenay, W. H. "Engendering Health: A Social Constructionist Examination of Men's Health Beliefs and Behaviors." *Psychology of Men and Masculinity,* 2000c, *1*, 4–15.

Courtenay, W. H. "Counseling Men in Medical Settings." In G. R. Brooks and G. E. Good (eds.), *The New Handbook of Psychotherapy and Counseling with Men: A Comprehensive Guide to Settings, Problems, and Treatment Approaches* (vol. 1). San Francisco: Jossey-Bass, 2001a.

Courtenay, W. H. "Men's Health: Ethnicity Matters." *Social Work Today,* 2001b, *1*(8), 20–22.

Courtenay, W. H. "A Global Perspective on the Field of Men's Health." *International Journal of Men's Health,* 2002, *1*(1), 1–13.

Courtenay, W. H. "Key Determinants of the Health and Well-Being of Men and Boys." *International Journal of Men's Health,* 2003, *2*(1), 1–30.

Courtenay, W. H., and Keeling, R. P. "Men, Gender, and Health: Toward an Interdisciplinary Approach." *Journal of American College Health,* 2000a, *48*(6), 1–4.

Courtenay, W. H. (guest ed.), and Keeling, R. P. (ed.). "Men's Health: A Theme Issue" [Special issue]. *Journal of American College Health,* 2000b, *48*(6).

Courtenay, W. H., McCreary, D. R., and Merighi, J. R. "Gender and Ethnic Differences in Health Beliefs and Behaviors." *Journal of Health Psychology,* 2002, *7*(3), 219–231.

Department of Health and Human Services (DHHS). "Deaths: Final Data for 1998." (DHHS publication no. PHS 2000–1120.) *National Vital Statistics Reports,* 48(11). Hyattsville, Md.: National Center for Health Statistics, 2000.

Harrington, N. G., and others. "Persuasive Strategies for Effective Anti-Drug Messages." *Communication Monographs,* 2003, 70(1), 16–38.

Keeling, R. P. "Social Norms Research in College Health." *Journal of American College Health,* 2000, 49(2), 53–56.

McCreary, D. R., Saucier, D. M., and Courtenay, W. H. "The Drive for Muscularity and Masculinity: Testing the Associations Among Gender Role Traits, Behaviors, Attitudes, and Conflict." *Psychology of Men and Masculinity,* forthcoming.

Morman, M. T. "Promoting the Testicular Self-Exam as a Preventative Health Care Strategy: Do Diagrams Make a Difference?" *International Journal of Men's Health,* 2002, 1(1), 73–88.

Patrick, M. S., Covin, J. R., Fulop, M., Calfas, K., and Lovato, C. "Health Risk Behaviors Among California College Students." *Journal of American College Health,* 1997, 45(6), 265–272.

Prochaska, J., Norcross, J., and DiClemente, C. *Changing for Good: The Revolutionary Program That Explains the Six Stages of Change and Teaches You How to Free Yourself from Bad Habits.* New York: Morrow, 1994.

Roter, D. L., and Hall, J. A. *Doctors Talking with Patients/Patients Talking with Doctors: Improving Communication in Medical Visits.* Westport, Conn.: Auburn House, 1997.

Stanton, A. L., and Courtenay, W. H. "Gender, Stress and Health." In R. H. Rozensky, N. G. Johnson, C. D. Goodheart, and R. Hammond (eds.), *Psychology Builds a Health World: Research and Practice Opportunities.* Washington, D.C.: American Psychological Association, 2003.

Zuckerman, M. *Behavioral Expressions and Biosocial Bases of Sensation Seeking.* New York: Cambridge University Press, 1994.

WILL H. COURTENAY *received his doctorate from the University of California, Berkeley, and is a licensed clinical social worker. He is founder and director of Men's Health Consulting and general editor of the* International Journal of Men's Health; *he teaches in the Department of Psychiatry and serves on the board of the McLean Hospital Center for Men at Harvard Medical School.*

This chapter presents a critical postmodern challenge to higher education professionals dealing with college men, their emotional development, and behavioral issues.

Arrested Emotional Development: Connecting College Men, Emotions, and Misconduct

Randall B. Ludeman

Higher education faces many challenges today, notably increased public scrutiny as the costs of postsecondary education increase. One need only read the newspapers and view the news on television to observe the attention being paid to the effectiveness and efficiency of the higher education system. It is clear that institutions will continue to be held more accountable for producing a quality product, meaning well-rounded, educated, productive, and civil citizens.

Most of us know that campus violence and behavioral issues have become a focus of attention and scrutiny. Many of us have read about issues such as sexual violence and harassment, abuse of alcohol and other drugs, rioting, and hate crimes. However, far too little research has been conducted to explore the role higher education can play in addressing and preventing these problems.

This chapter presents a critical postmodern challenge to higher education professionals dealing specifically with college men and behavioral issues. The information presented is a result of a qualitative inquiry into current judicial practices and male students' experiences in the college judicial process. The inquiry included a content analysis of selected judicial documents, Websites, and other materials. In addition, data were analyzed from college men's campus judicial experiences.

The chapter begins with a review of the issues of hegemonic masculinity and behavior. Next, the effects of the male socialization process on

New Directions for Student Services, no. 107, Fall 2004 © Wiley Periodicals, Inc.

male behavior are explored. The third section presents recommendations for connecting with men's emotional development as a significant component of resolving behavioral challenges. The chapter concludes with a summary of the issues.

The Problem: Men and Behavior

It is easier (and riskier) than ever to write about the dark side of male behavior. After centuries of celebrating male patriarchal manhood, a new gender consciousness has arisen. Feminist scholarship has written women back into history, highlighting the former marginality of women and challenging the misogyny that is deeply imbedded in Western culture (Brooks and Silverstein, 1995).

Research regarding men and behavior has often focused on men and violence (for example, Berkowitz, 1992; Good, Hepper, Hillenbrand-Gunn, and Wang, 1995; Hong, 2000; Marshall, 1993). Much of this research has focused on men's violent or oppressive behavior against women (for example, Berkowitz, 1994; Rhoads, 1995; Sanday, 1990). Many authors have written about the disproportionate overrepresentation of men as both perpetrators and victims of violence (for example, Brooks and Silverstein, 1995; Diamond, 1994; Hong, 2000; Pollack, 1998; Seidler, 1996). Research has suggested men most often are the perpetrators of homicide (USDHHS, 1991), physical assaults (Valois and irothers, 1993), sexual assaults (Koss, Gidycz, and Wisniewski, 1987), domestic abuse (Federal Bureau of Investigation, 1992), and bias-related crimes (Levin, 1993). Boys and men are more likely than girls and women to bear weapons (Courtenay, 1998; Hong, 2000), which significantly increases their risk for violence. Men have also been cited as a significant proportion of the victims of violence (Hong, 2000). It has become abundantly clear, as stated by Brooks and Silverstein (1995), that "male violence represents the darkest feature of masculinity" (p. 282).

A growing number of researchers and authors have argued that male violence has been prescribed by the traditional masculine norms of hegemonic masculinity (for example, Brooks and Silverstein, 1995; Courtenay, 1998; Hong, 2000; Pollack, 1998). Creating what Brooks and Silverstein (1995) called the "dark side of masculinity" (p. 281), traditional masculine roles and norms have been purported to encourage behavior such as violence, sexual abuse and sexual harassment, substance abuse and other self-destructive behaviors, relationship inadequacies, absent fathering, and social-emotional withdrawal. These dark-side behaviors commonly have been regarded as the problem of only a few deviant men; however, it has been argued more recently that these behaviors actually may "exist to a lesser degree in the normative masculine role socialization of all men" (Brooks and Silverstein, 1995, p. 281).

There is little published research dealing specifically with college students' behavior, and most of what does exist is primarily based on studies done before 1980 (Dannells, 1997). The research regarding disruptive college student behavior typically has focused on the effectiveness of judicial programs and services. However, several studies have focused on the characteristics of college student offenders. Dannells (1997) reported that a consistent profile of students involved with disciplinary problems was "immature, impulsive young men, most often freshmen and sophomores, who have not developed positive feelings toward the institution and who very likely were engaged in alcohol use or abuse at the time of the incident" (p. 28). Van Kuren and Creamer (1989) reported that students whose parents have college degrees were less likely to violate student codes of conduct than were students whose parents did not have college degrees. They also found that "students who had positive feelings about the institution, in general, were less likely to be offenders" (p. 264).

Alcohol abuse has been linked to behavior problems on college campuses (Dannells, 1997). Hanson and Engs (1995) reported that campus administrators indicated alcohol was increasingly involved in violations of campus policy and in violent behavior. Wechsler, Deutsch, and Dowdall (1995) found that at campuses where binge drinking is common, 87 percent of the nonbinge drinkers who lived on campus reported they were affected adversely by the binge drinking of others.

Dannells and Stuber (1992) reported that psychopathology appears to be on the rise among college students, leading to more pathological origins of student misconduct. This explanation of student misbehavior is supported by the apparent increase in frequency of behaviors such as sexual harassment, acquaintance rape, dating and domestic violence, alcohol abuse, and stalking (Gallagher, Harmon, and Lingenfelter, 1994).

The men's studies movement has also brought to light the issues surrounding men's problematic behavior. "Scholars from the men's studies movement have documented a clear link between socialization into stereotypical norms of hegemonic masculinity and an increased risk for experiencing violence" (Hong, 2000, p. 269). However, many college campuses have failed to recognize this link between men, socialization, and violence and have relied only on traditional approaches to violence prevention (Hong, 2000). In the college setting, the judicial system is the venue for handling disruptive behavior, including incidents of violence. It would seem beneficial, therefore, for student affairs practitioners and male college students to understand better how gender roles and socialization affect male students in the collegiate environment in order to proactively intervene at early stages of misconduct to prevent increasingly disruptive patterns of behavior.

It is evident that more research is needed regarding the origins of student misconduct and appropriate institutional intervention strategies. In addition, little research has focused on the developmental outcomes of student judicial processes. Although the literature regarding student judicial affairs does include reference to the importance of student development and learning (for example, Dannells, 1991, 1997), specific structures and processes for providing student development and learning in the judicial arena are absent.

In examining the behavioral problems of college men, it seems significant to understand better how the socialization of boys and men contributes to these problems. In particular, emotional development appears to have a significant relationship to behavioral difficulties experienced by college men.

Male Gender Role Socialization

> In the United States a real boy climbs trees, disdains girls, dirties his knees, plays with soldiers, and takes blue for his favorite color. When they go to school, real boys prefer manual training, gym, and arithmetic. In college the boys smoke pipes, drink beer, and major in engineering or physics. The real boy matures into a "man's man" who plays poker, goes hunting, drinks brandy, and dies in war (Brown, 1965).

The male gender role is established early for boys. Society places a unique set of expectations on boys to deal autonomously with life, hide pain, and avoid behavior that shames themselves or family (Pollack, 1999). Pollack (1998, 1999) described boys as experiencing "gender straitjackets," which affect them by forcing repression of emotions and needs for love and affection. "Confused by society's mixed messages about what's expected of them as boys, and later as men, many feel a sadness and disconnection they cannot even name" (Pollack, 1998, p. xxi). As a result, it is often difficult for us to notice when boys are experiencing difficulty. Yet research shows boys are experiencing crises in many ways: "Boys are failing at school, succeeding at suicide, engaging in homicide, and disconnecting from their own inner lives: losing their genuine voices and selves" (Pollack, 1999, p. 7).

Boys are influenced by parents, other adults, and peers to behave differently from girls. Boys are more likely to be encouraged to play aggressively (Hyde and Linn, 1986) and to be punished physically for inappropriate behavior (Hartley, 1974). Parents and peers are more likely to discourage behavior that diverges from prescribed gender norms (Fagot, 1985). Expressing emotion, such as crying, is discouraged by adult men (often fathers), who remind boys that only girls cry (Rabinowitz and Cochran, 1994). Television and other media portray male heroes as possessing strength, determination, and dominance (Greenberg, 1982). The messages begin early for boys that they should adhere to the traditional masculine code.

The socialization process has been purported to hinder the emotional development of boys and men. For many males, "one striking and far-reaching consequence of the male socialization ordeal is an inability to differentiate and identify their emotions" (Levant, 1997, p. 9). Levant (1997) has labeled this condition "normative male alexithymia" (p. 9), which is the inability for men to put feelings into words or even to be aware of them. According to Levant (1997), the condition, in conjunction with the socialization of boys to suppress tender, vulnerable, and caring feelings, leaves only aggression and sexuality as accepted channels for the release of emotional energy.

As boys grow up and enter adulthood, society challenges them to develop further their identity, traditionally associated with the important tasks of choosing an occupation and establishing intimate relationships (Levinson and others, 1978). For young men choosing to attend a college or university, entering the adult world can often be delayed. These men can explore and experiment with relationships, academic study, and work without assuming much of the responsibility of being an adult (Rabinowitz and Cochran, 1994). However, these college men are faced with the development of competence, learning to manage emotions, developing autonomy, establishing an identity, freeing interpersonal relationships, developing a purpose, and developing integrity (Chickering, 1969; Chickering and Reisser, 1993). These developmental tasks may conflict with their socialized experience and expectations of masculinity.

In facing these developmental tasks, college men find expression of emotion and other traditionally defined feminine qualities more desirable and beneficial (Levinson and others, 1978). Expression of feminine qualities has been shown to create conflict for men; therefore, college-aged men are likely to experience difficulty in expressing concern for others, disclosing vulnerabilities, and describing their feelings to others (Cournoyer and Mahalik, 1995). The fear of femininity in fact is central to the theory of male gender role conflict purported by O'Neil (1981a, 1981b, 1982, 1990).

Research focused on the effects of socially defined expectations of masculinity on boys and men frequently has centered on the concept of male gender role conflict (MGRC). O'Neil (1990) described gender role conflict as occurring when "rigid, sexist, or restricted gender roles learned during socialization result in the personal restriction, devaluation, or violation of others or self" (p. 25). O'Neil theorized that traditional male role socialization produces contradictory and unrealistic messages that lead to a fear of femininity (O'Neil, 1981a, 1981b, 1982). As a result, men may engage in patterns of gender role conflict from fear of becoming or appearing feminine (Cournoyer and Mahalik, 1995; Rhoads, 1995).

MGRC has been found to create liabilities for college men that include self-destructive behaviors (Meth, 1990), increased stress (Stewart and Lykes, 1985), disregard for health (Courtenay, 1998; Nathanson, 1977), substance abuse and addiction (Blazina and Watkins, 1996; Capraro, 2000), and increased depression and anxiety (Sharpe and Heppner, 1991).

If the male socialization process indeed shapes or restricts the emotional skills and development of boys and men, then it seems likely that the demands of the college environment will create challenges for men related to their relationships and experiences on the college campus. Understanding the impact of hegemonic masculinity on male college students is important in delivery of effective student services.

Working with Men and Emotions to Resolve Behavioral Issues

As student development practitioners become more aware of the effects of hegemonic masculinity, we may be better able to assess current judicial affairs practices and make necessary changes in the provision of these practices. Judicial processes, though serving the function of accountability for behavior, can also create opportunities for emotional growth and development. Judicial officers must foster an awareness of the emotional development of college men. Judicial officers must also understand their own emotional needs and development in order to effectively role model and facilitate discussions with college men related to emotions. For college men to understand possible reasons for their inappropriate choices and behaviors, the judicial process venue must be open to men's exploration of their emotionality and its connection to their behavioral choices. This means incorporating emotional work with students into the judicial process.

Although judicial programs often refer to empathy and learning as essential to the judicial process and outcomes, evidence of how the judicial process promotes these elements is rarely presented. For example, referrals to counseling are common as outcomes of judicial proceedings, but the actual process of counseling is sometimes suggested to occur away from the judicial process. Judicial programs usually incorporate the use of educational sanctions. These sanctions may be referrals to learning experiences that also occur away from the judicial process. This would suggest student development and learning are actually desirable supplements to the judicial process rather than a central concern.

Consistent with Smith's notion (1987) of the existence of gender-specific work roles in society, judicial processes appear to separate functions related to the work of providing judicial services. Smith (1987) suggested that "feminine" work often cleans up, tidies, and allows the "masculine" (main) work to proceed: "The place of women. . . . is where the work is done to facilitate men's occupation of the conceptual mode of action. Women keep house, bear and care for children, look after men when they are sick, and in general provide for the logistics of their bodily existence. . . . At almost every point women mediate for men the relation between the conceptual mode of action and the actual concrete forms on which it depends" (Smith, 1987, p. 83).

The separation of gender work roles appears to be present in campus judicial processes. Judicial professionals are expected to be sensitive to the developmental needs of college students, but this more emotionally related "feminine" work appears to be a responsibility delegated outside the judicial arena, as if it were not so important as the primary "masculine" work of adjudicating misbehavior. If judicial processes and outcomes are intended to be developmental, empathic, and respectful, we must then incorporate these philosophies into the actual practices we carry out. Ideally, this would include giving students an opportunity to explore their emotional awareness and expressiveness during their judicial experience, rather than as a supplemental and subsequent process.

It would seem beneficial for student development and judicial affairs professionals to recognize the overwhelming perceptions students have of the judicial process as adversarial. The judicial process is power-laden in that the institution has authority to administer a code of conduct and to hold students accountable to a set of behavioral expectations. Students entering the judicial process often feel they have less knowledge than the administrators responsible for facilitating the process, and as discussed by Foucault (1980) knowledge is a technology of power. As students perceive this power differential, the judicial process milieu may not be conducive to student development and learning in general, and emotional development in particular. Empowering students through creating opportunities to learn about judicial processes prior to participating in them may lessen the perceived power imbalance and result in a more developmental experience for these students.

Gehring (2001) discussed the incompatibility of the legalistic nature of judicial process in higher education and the student development outcomes they intend to provide: "The disciplinary process on campuses has been too procedural and mirrors an adversarial proceeding that precludes student development" (p. 466). Gehring suggested that higher education has allowed "creeping legalism" (Dannells, 1997, p. 69) to bring the due process rights and procedures way beyond what is required by the courts, and that campuses must review their disciplinary procedures to bring back the focus on education and student development.

Many judicial programs espouse a philosophy that refers to procedures that are empathic and supportive of students participating in these processes. However, this discourse often competes and conflicts with the legalistic discourse, which may confuse students and staff members participating in the processes. Both these principles are deemed important, but it appears that the discourses of legal versus developmental philosophy compete for status. Rather than complementing each other, these contested discourses have become a binary argument (Lather, 1991), with each discourse vying for hegemonic status in the judicial arena. These contested discourses have created tensions among judicial affairs practitioners.

Chickering (1969) theorized that learning to manage and express emotions effectively is a major developmental task for college-aged students. Student development professionals must recognize the importance of the emotional experience of college men and develop systems and processes that encourage emotional exploration, expression, and development.

If college men view the judicial process as a power-laden, adversarial process, they are less likely to experience a willingness to explore and express their emotions.

Several possible judicial venues could be explored in relation to enhancing the emotional development of male college students. For example, mediation as a venue for resolution of judicial complaints empowers both the complainant and the accused students to learn from their experience. Serr and Taber (1987) stated that "in the collegiate setting, mediation provides an educational, nonadversarial method of resolving conflict" (p. 83). Warters (1995) also discussed mediation as an educational approach to conflict resolution on college campuses. The goal of mediation is to empower the disputing parties to generate alternatives regarding a resolution to their dispute (Serr and Taber, 1987).

Through the less adversarial process of mediation, judicial officers could encourage emotional awareness and expressiveness on the part of the male students, and facilitate emotional development and learning through challenging and empathic processes. The mediator, whether a judicial officer or another trained professional, could more readily incorporate a counseling style and approach in resolving conflict or conduct code violations as well as pay specific attention to opportunities for students' emotional needs and growth during the process. Through role modeling emotional expression and encouraging and affirming emotional expression by male students, male mediators in particular could afford college men opportunities to successfully cross gender borders of emotionality. For example, two roommates who engaged in a fight in the residence halls could be brought together through mediation to discuss their emotions related to the conflict and the altercation. The mediator could work with these men to explore how their emotional awareness and expressiveness, or lack thereof, contributed to the conflict. Through the mediation process these men could be empowered to develop insight as to how they can better understand and manage their emotions.

A second recommendation for the developmental processing of college student behavioral concerns would be to employ a restorative justice model, which involves the victims' and accused students' peers in the resolution of judicial cases. Restorative justice enables offenders to make amends to their victims and the community; builds offender and victim skills; and involves the offender, victim, and community in the process and resolution (DeVore and Gentilcore, 1999). This restorative justice model has been used as a venue for addressing at-risk youth (for example, DeVore and Gentilcore, 1999) and community-based moral education (for example, Schweigert, 1999).

A restorative justice model could be valuable in enabling college students to better understand their emotions and behavior. For example, if a male student is charged with creating excessive noise late at night on a residence hall floor, the students affected by this disruption on the floor could be brought together to engage in a process of determining the judicial outcomes. During this process, the judicial officer could encourage all students involved to explore aspects of the case, including their emotional experiences before, during, and following the incident. As emotions are recognized and expressed by these students, the judicial officer could facilitate a developmental discussion in order to acknowledge the relationship between emotions and behavior.

Another venue for facilitating male students' emotional development is a group process for male students who have participated in the judicial process. During this group process, judicial officers could share observations with these men related to their emotional awareness and expressiveness prior to and during the judicial process. Discussions regarding the consequences of gender role conflict, hegemonic masculinity, and restricted emotionality could be presented and discussed. Most important, judicial officers could promote a supportive environment that is conducive to emotional awareness and expressiveness. Rather than referring these students to a service venue away from the judicial system, judicial officers could be educated and trained to provide emotionally developmental experiences as an extension of the judicial process.

Conclusions

Judicial affairs professionals and students have expressed concerns with the legalistic philosophy adopted by campus judicial programs. Legislative initiatives and new policies from governing boards have provided structure to student judicial programs and services and will continue to do so (Bostic and Gonzalez, 1999), but professionals must persist in advocating for a process that both addresses the legal requirements and is focused on student development and learning. In addition, more research is needed to explore the effects of legalistic and developmental philosophies on the educational outcomes of judicial processes.

College men are likely to experience the effects of hegemonic masculinity. The gender border existing for these men may reinforce their restricted emotionality. Current judicial practices may also fail to establish a venue conducive to the emotional development of college men. Further complicating the judicial venue is the legalistic nature of judicial process, which lends a perception of a process that is adversarial at heart.

It seems imperative that we engage in a review of current judicial standards, philosophies, and structures. We must recognize the power relations we have created through current practices and reframe our vision of judicial affairs to be more conducive to student development and learning. Particularly for college men, the influences of hegemonic masculinity, gender role conflict, and restricted emotionality must be recognized, and judicial practices must be designed to challenge these existing difficulties for college men. Practitioners may benefit from drawing upon men's studies for understanding the issues of men's emotional development and behavioral issues. By empowering male students to cross gender borders and explore a broader range of emotional awareness and expressiveness, we may stimulate for these men "a self-sustaining process of critical analysis and enlightened action" (Lather, 1991, p. 75).

References

Berkowitz, A. "College Men as Perpetrators of Acquaintance Rape and Sexual Assault: A Review of Recent Research." *Journal of American College Health,* 1992, *40,* 175–181.

Berkowitz, A. *Men and Rape: Theory, Research and Prevention Programs in Higher Education.* San Francisco: Jossey-Bass, 1994.

Blazina, C., and Watkins, C. E. "Masculine Gender Role Conflict: Effects on College Men's Psychological Well-Being, Chemical Substance Usage, and Attitudes Toward Help-Seeking." *Journal of Counseling Psychology,* 1996, *43*(4), 461–465.

Bostic, D., and Gonzalez, G. "Practices, Opinions, Knowledge, and Recommendations from Judicial Officers in Public Higher Education." *NASPA Journal,* 1999, *36*(3), 166–183.

Brooks, G. R., and Silverstein, L. B. "Understanding the Dark Side of Masculinity: An Interactive Systems Model." In R. Levant and W. Pollack (eds.), *A New Psychology of Men.* New York: Basic Books, 1995.

Brown, R. *Social Psychology.* New York: Free Press, 1965.

Capraro, R. L. "Why College Men Drink: Alcohol, Adventure, and the Paradox of Masculinity." *Journal of American College Health,* 2000, *48,* 307–315.

Chickering, A. W. *Education and Identity* (1st ed.). San Francisco: Jossey-Bass, 1969.

Chickering, A. W., and Reisser, L. *Education and Identity* (2nd ed.). San Francisco: Jossey-Bass, 1993.

Cournoyer, R. J., and Mahalik, J. R. "Cross-sectional Study of Gender Role Conflict Examining College-aged and Middle-aged Men. *Journal of Counseling Psychology,* 1995, *42,* 11–19.

Courtenay, W. H. "College Men's Health: An Overview and a Call to Action." *Journal of American College Health,* 1998, *46,* 279–287.

Dannells, M. D. "Changes in Student Misconduct and Institutional Response Over 10 Years." *Journal of College Student Development,* 1991, *32,* 166–170.

Dannells, M. D. *From Discipline to Development: Rethinking Student Conduct in Higher Education.* ASHE-ERIC Higher Education Report, vol. 25, no. 2. Washington, D.C.: Graduate School of Education and Human Development, George Washington University, 1997.

Dannells, M. D., and Stuber, D. "Mandatory Psychiatric Withdrawal of Severely Disturbed Students: A Study and Policy Recommendation." *NASPA Journal,* 1992, *29,* 163–168.

DeVore, D., and Gentilcore, K. "Balanced and Restorative Justice and Educational Programming for Youth at Risk." *Clearing House,* 1999, *73*(2), 96–100.

Diamond, J. *The Warrior's Journey Home: Healing Men, Healing the Planet.* Oakland, Calif.: New Harbinger, 1994.

Fagot, B. "A Cautionary Note: Parent's Socialization of Boys and Girls." *Sex Roles,* 1985, *12,* 471–476.

Federal Bureau of Investigation. *Uniform Crime Reports.* Washington, D.C.: U. S. Government Printing Office, 1992.

Foucault, M. *Power/Knowledge* (C. Gordon and others, trans.). New York: Pantheon, 1980.

Gallagher, R. P., Harmon, W. W, and Lingenfelter, C. O. "CSAOs' Perceptions of the Changing Incidence of Problematic College Student Behavior." *NASPA Journal,* 1994, *32,* 37–45.

Gehring, D. D. "The Objectives of Student Discipline and the Process That's Due: Are They Compatible?" *NASPA Journal,* 2001, *38*(4), 466–481.

Good, G., Hepper, M., Hillenbrand-Gunn, T., and Wang, L. "Sexual and Psychological Violence: An Exploratory Study of Predictors in College Men." *Journal of Men's Studies,* 1995, *4,* 59–71.

Greenberg, B. "Television and Role Socialization: An Overview." In National Institute of Mental Health, *Television and Behavior: Ten Years of Scientific Progress and Implications for the Eighties.* Washington, D.C.: U.S. Government Printing Office, 1982.

Hanson, D. J., and Engs, R. C. "College Drinking: Administrator Perceptions, Campus Policies, and Student Behaviors." *NASPA Journal,* 1995, *32,* 106–114.

Hartley, R. "Sex-Role Pressures and the Socialization of the Male Child." In J. Pleck and J. Sawyer (eds.), *Men and Masculinity.* Upper Saddle River, N.J.: Prentice Hall, 1974.

Hong, L. "Toward a Transformed Approach to Prevention: Breaking the Link Between Masculinity and Violence." *Journal of American College Health,* 2000, *48,* 269–279.

Hyde, J., and Linn, M. *The Psychology of Gender.* Baltimore, Md.: Johns Hopkins University Press, 1986.

Koss, M., Gidycz, C., and Wisniewski, N. "The Scope of Rape: Incidence and Prevalence of Sexual Aggression and Victimization in a National Sample of Higher Education Students." *Journal of Consulting and Clinical Psychology,* 1987, *55,* 162–170.

Lather, P. *Getting Smart: Feminist Research and Pedagogy with/in the Postmodern.* New York: Routledge, 1991.

Levant, R. F. *Men and Emotions: A Psychoeducational Approach.* New York: Newbridge, 1997.

Levin, B. "A Dream Deferred: The Social and Legal Implications of Hate Crimes in the 1990s." *Journal of Intergroup Relations,* 1993, *9,* 3–27.

Levinson, D. J., Darrow, C. N., Klein, E. B., Levinson, M. H., and McKee, B. *The Seasons of a Man's Life.* New York: Knopf, 1978.

Marshall, D. "Violence and the Male Gender Role." *Journal of College Student Psychotherapy,* 1993, *8,* 203–218.

Meth, R. L. "The Road to Masculinity." In R. L. Meth and R. S. Pasick (eds.), *Men in Therapy: The Challenge of Change.* New York: Guilford Press, 1990.

Nathanson, C. A. "Sex Roles as Variables in Preventative Health Behavior." *Journal of Community Health,* 1977, *3,* 142–155.

O'Neil, J. M. "Male Sex-Role Conflicts, Sexism, and Masculinity: Psychological Implications for Men, Women, and the Counseling Psychologist." *Counseling Psychologist,* 1981a, *9,* 61–81.

O'Neil, J. M. "Patterns of Gender Role Conflict and Strain: Sexism and Fear of Femininity in Men's Lives." *Personnel and Guidance Journal,* 1981b, *60,* 203–210.

O'Neil, J. M. "Gender Role Conflict and Strain in Men's Lives: Implications for Psychiatrists, Psychologists, and Other Human Service Providers." In K. Solomon and N. B. Levy (eds.), *Men in Transition: Changing Male Roles, Theory, and Therapy.* New York: Plenum, 1982.

O'Neil, J. M. "Assessing Men's Gender Role Conflict." In D. Moore and F. Leafgren (eds.), *Problem Solving Strategies and Interventions for Men in Conflict.* Alexandria, Va.: American Counseling Association, 1990.

Pollack, W. S. *Real Boys: Rescuing Our Sons from the Myths of Boyhood.* New York: Holt, 1998.

Pollack, W. S. "The Sacrifice of Isaac: Toward a New Psychology of Boys and Men." *Society for the Psychological Study of Men and Masculinity Bulletin,* 1999, *4*(1), 7–14.

Rabinowitz, F. E., and Cochran, S. V. *Man Alive: A Primer of Men's Issues.* Pacific Grove, Calif.: Brooks/Cole, 1994.

Rhoads, R. A. "Whale Tales, Dog Piles, and Beer Goggles: An Ethnographic Case Study of Fraternity Life." *Anthropology and Education Quarterly,* 1995, *26*(3), 306–323.

Sanday, P. *Fraternity Gang Rape: Sex, Brotherhood, and Privilege on Campus.* New York: New York University, 1990.

Schweigert, F. J. "Learning the Common Good: Principles of Community-Based Moral Education in Restorative Justice." *Journal of Moral Education,* 1999, *28*(2), 163–183.

Seidler, V. "Masculinity and Violence." In L. May, R. A. Strikwerda, and P. D. Hopkins (eds.), *Rethinking Masculinity: Philosophical Explorations in Light of Feminism.* Lanham, Md.: Rowman and Littlefield, 1996.

Serr, R. L., and Taber, R. S. "Mediation: A Judicial Affairs Alternative." In R. Caruso and W. Travelstead (eds.), *Enhancing Campus Judicial Systems.* San Francisco: Jossey-Bass, 1987.

Sharpe, M. J., and Heppner, P. P. "Gender Role, Gender Role Conflict, and Psychological Well-Being in Men." *Journal of Counseling Psychology,* 1991, *38,* 323–330.

Smith, D. E. *The Everyday World as Problematic: A Feminist Sociology.* Boston: Northeastern University Press, 1987.

Stewart, A. J., and Lykes, M. B. (eds.). *Gender and Personality: Current Perspectives on Theory and Research.* Durham, N.C.: Duke University Press, 1985.

U.S. Department of Health and Human Services (DHHS). *Healthy People 2000: National Health Promotion and Disease Prevention Objectives.* (DHHS publication no. 91–50212.) Washington, D.C.: U.S. Department of Health and Human Services, 1991.

Valois, R., Vincent, M., McKeown, R., Garrison, C., and Kirby, S. "Adolescent Risk Behaviors and the Potential for Violence: A Look at What's Coming to Campus." *Journal of American College Health,* 1993, *41,* 141–147.

Van Kuren, N. F., and Creamer, D. G. "The Conceptualization and Testing of a Causal Model of College Student Disciplinary Status." *Journal of College Student Development,* 1989, *30,* 257–265.

Warters, W. C. "Conflict Management in Higher Education: A Review of Current Approaches." In S. A. Holton (ed.), *Conflict Resolution in Higher Education.* New Directions for Higher Education, no. 92. San Francisco: Jossey-Bass, 1995.

Wechsler, H., Deutsch, C., and Dowdall, G. "Too Many Colleges Still in Denial About Alcohol Abuse." *Chronicle of Higher Education,* Apr. 14, 1995, pp. B1–2.

RANDALL B. LUDEMAN received his Ph.D. from Iowa State University and is associate director of residential life and adjunct instructor of gender studies at Bemidji State University (Minnesota).

7

Innovative programs in male spirituality can help college men challenge conventional masculine gender roles and envision creative ways of being men.

Men, Spirituality, and the Collegiate Experience

W. Merle Longwood, Mark W. Muesse,
William Schipper, O.S.B.

Despite their dominance of religious institutions, American men generally have been uneasy with spirituality. In the nineteenth and twentieth centuries, debates about masculinity often centered on whether atheism or Christianity was the more "manly" viewpoint (Kirkley, 1996). Proponents argued that atheism was a more appropriate philosophy for men because the church was "feminized" and numerically dominated by women, and because religious belief tended to make males sentimental, weak, and "soft-minded." The advocates of "muscular Christianity" countered with the argument that men could be both pious and masculine. That the issue was even a matter of debate demonstrates both the unease American men often have with religion as well as their anxieties about their own masculinity. In the twenty-first century, there is evidence that this uneasiness is still current. One of the popular slogans of the Promise Keepers, the evangelical men's organization, is "Real Men Love Jesus." If men were truly comfortable with loving Jesus, asserting that this is something real men do would not be necessary. It is hard to imagine that one would come across the corresponding motto, "Real Women Love Jesus."

One need not look far to understand why American men are ambivalent about religion. The ideals of masculinity encourage males to be independent, controlling, rational, self-sufficient, active, emotionally restrictive, and competitive. Certainly not all men live up to these ideals, but they are the basic standards by which one's masculinity is frequently judged. The domains of spirituality and religion, however, often advocate qualities that are at odds with dominant masculine values. The spiritual realm tends to prize interiority, yielding, cooperation, connectedness, emotionality, and community. It is little wonder that despite the dominance of men in leadership positions, far more women than men participate in American religious institutions. Religiously active men, even those in leadership, are often regarded with suspicion by other men, almost as if they constituted a third gender category. Theologian James Nelson recalls seeing the restrooms in a Swedish church designated for "women," "men," and "clergy" (personal communication with authors, April 1995). By the standards of conventional American masculinity, the manliness of religious men, especially overtly religious men, may be in doubt. As if to assuage concerns about the masculinity of their participants, the Promise Keepers conduct their rallies in that most masculine of venues, the football stadium.

The standards of American masculinity thus make it difficult for college men to acknowledge their spiritual natures to others, especially to other men. Yet research clearly indicates that spirituality is vitally important to the great majority of them (Young, 2003; Miller, Ryan, and Laurence, 2001; Chickering, 2004; Herndon, 2003; Bennett, 2004; Sax, 2004). Compounding the situation is the fact that most colleges and universities, as bastions of secularity, do little to acknowledge and nurture the spiritualities of young people. The academic programs of most schools rarely even hint at the idea that human beings have a spiritual dimension, much less endeavor to address and develop it. The areas where spirituality is addressed—namely, chaplaincies and programs run by local churches and denominations—tend to be marginal, sectarian, and too traditionally religious for many students. Thus, when men enter American institutions of higher learning they labor under the strain of the standards of conventional masculinity and find an entire aspect of their lives unrecognized and underdeveloped. Both the neglect of spirituality and the uncritical acceptance of dominant masculine ideals, we contend, do much to distort men as whole human beings and bring much unhappiness to their lives.

Developing spirituality and addressing burdensome masculine standards are goals that can be effectively accomplished through innovative programs that bring men together in small groups to reflect on their lives. The exploration and development of spirituality in men's groups is an implicit challenge to conventional masculine norms and a crucible for envisioning new ways of being male. At the same time, the critical scrutiny of traditional masculinity frees men to enhance their spiritual dimensions by challenging the beliefs that would have them regard spirituality as unworthy of "real" men. To show the great potential benefit of male spiritual development, we turn to describe an especially effective model established at Saint John's University.

Men's Spirituality Groups at Saint John's University

Saint John's University (SJU), a college for men founded in 1857 by Benedictine men, has a coordinate relationship with the College of Saint Benedict, a college for women founded in 1913 by Benedictine women. Though maintaining separate residential campuses where monastic women and men are involved in the life of students on a daily basis, the two schools share a single academic program with coeducational classes.

In 1995, Gar Kellom, vice president of student development at Saint John's, gathered together a group of eight monks from Saint John's Abbey to consider the question, "What contribution can a Benedictine community of men make in the area of men's development?" The group quickly centered on the critical question of men's spirituality and decided to devote a year to understanding their own spiritualities through sharing their spiritual autobiographies. This experience had such a powerful effect that they decided to form similar groups for SJU students, using their group experience as a prototype. In 1997 two student spirituality groups were begun. It soon became apparent that students had the same positive experience as the monks had, and new groups were established.

The Formation of Men's Spirituality Groups

Today, all entering students at Saint John's are invited to join a spirituality group through an informational dinner bringing together prospective and active group members. Of course, not all students accept the invitation, but many do.

Group Meetings

Group size is limited to ten students and two facilitators. At the first meeting, facilitators emphasize the importance of confidentiality, commitment, and communication. Confidentiality is essential to building trust in the group, and it is stressed from the outset. Members are also asked to commit to stay with the same group throughout their college years. They are asked to communicate as honestly and openly as they feel comfortable. As much as possible, they are encouraged to talk in the first person, taking personal ownership of feelings, fears, learning, and experiences.

Groups meet every two or three weeks for about an hour. Each meeting centers on one member who presents his story to initiate the discussion. At the end of his presentation, other members may ask questions for clarification.

This arrangement allows young men the chance to discuss serious personal matters beyond the topics of sports, politics, and sex (the usual range of masculine subjects). It also allows group members to reflect on how another man's story has triggered reactions within themselves, allowing them to grasp that they often have the same fears, joys, and challenges as their peers.

Group Development over the Collegiate Career

During each of the four years of the group's existence, members reflect on a specific theme appropriate to their stage of spiritual and educational development. In the first year, groups discuss the topic "Who I am and what I believe." Each member has one meeting to tell his story. The two facilitators are generally the first to present during this year and thereby model the process.

The second year is devoted to relationships. Each member reflects on how his beliefs and self-understanding influence his relationships.

During the third year, members go deeper in the areas of most interest to the group. Some groups take up the theme of authenticity; others consider the topic of beauty; still others continue with the topic of relationships.

Year four is devoted to articulating what has been learned through the group experience and process.

Assessment of the Program's Effectiveness

Shortly after the men's spirituality group program was begun, two of us (Longwood and Muesse) were asked to serve as outside, independent evaluators and consultants. In 1999 we began a series of annual visits to Saint John's to interview students, facilitators, and administrators to assess the effectiveness of the groups in helping students meet the university's mission to foster the intellectual and spiritual development of men. We formulated a set of questions based on our work in men's studies and the university's Benedictine tradition to evaluate the program's success in five interrelated areas. Specifically, we wanted to know how the groups influenced participants' (1) self-understanding as men, (2) relationships with others outside the group, (3) sense of spirituality, (4) sense of justice and compassion, and (5) sense of vocation. Although there are certainly differences among the groups since each group takes on a personality of its own, it is possible to make some generalizations about the experiences of men in these groups.

Self-Understanding as a Man. Throughout the groups, the men said that participation had given them the opportunity to speak about things that men do not usually talk about with other men. They frequently commented that their closest friends were men outside the group, but it was within the group that they were able to be the most open and honest about the important problems and issues in their lives. They expressed appreciation for how the facilitators (who in almost all cases were monks) modeled how to communicate. Members of freshmen groups characteristically acknowledged that it was valuable to talk with other men about topics that were "deeper" than conversations about "sports or girls." By opening up issues about the male role, the groups foster candidness and sensitivity, thus helping to "normalize" intimacy among men, as one sophomore put it. Members of the senior groups elaborated more fully what they had learned during four years of participation, including the value of listening, the value of hearing other men's stories, and the importance of a redefined masculinity, to the point where they viewed masculinity as largely a social construction. Thus the groups help break down the cultural gender binds that encourage men to believe that being stereotypically masculine is the only authentic form of manhood.

Life and Relationships Outside the Group. The men in all the groups indicated that their involvement had had a positive effect on their relationships outside the group, as they became more sensitive to relationship issues and gained insight listening to others talk about their relationships. They frequently commented that being part of a group had helped them understand their fathers better, and they believed that their relationships with their fathers had improved as a result, often suggesting that they were now able to discuss significant issues together. Others observed that their relationships with both parents and siblings had improved, and that they themselves had learned to be more empathic, skillful listeners and expressive within their families. Many men indicated that being in the groups had made them more comfortable talking with others as individuals and in groups. On campus, they indicated that being in a group had helped them in their relationships with women as well as with other men. They perceived that the women on campus appreciated their involvement in a spirituality group and that other "Johnnies" were often envious of their participation.

Sense of Spirituality and Connection to God, the Universe, and Others. In all the groups, the participants expressed enthusiasm about how they had been able to focus on spirituality, which they defined broadly and distinguished from institutional religion. They perceived the groups they participated in as being religiously diverse, which they viewed as a benefit. They frequently observed that it was a "nice surprise" to discover that the monks were accepting of them as young men and easy to talk to, even about women. The men expressed amazement at the variety of spiritualities among the men in their groups, while at the same time they were impressed by the similarities. An individual who regarded himself as an atheist felt free to acknowledge his beliefs, emphasizing how his group had enabled its participants to express their spirituality without any judgment by others. Being comfortable with one's own spirituality, he said, leads to being comfortable with others' spirituality. Other men expressed gratitude that their groups had supported them in their expression of spirituality apart from church. On the other hand, other men frequently commented on the benefit of learning about the spirituality of the monks, which helped them break down stereotypes about the monks as well as about the Catholic religion. Many men indicated how good it was to know that others are also serious about their faith. Few talked about spirituality in relation to "the universe" but instead related spirituality to their own inner development and their interpersonal relationships.

Sense of Justice and Compassion for Others and the Earth. Few of the men in any of the groups emphasized justice concerns beyond interpersonal relationships, although in one of the groups some of the men reflected on what it means to take care of the members of one's community and how their involvement in the group had given them deeper insights into the nature and function of communities. In one group, it became clear that discussions about social justice had been an important, animating dynamic in their group experience, as conversations—and outright debates—revolved around two members of the group, one of whom was described by another student as the campus "Mr. Social Justice" while the other was a cadet in ROTC. Students in other groups indicated that they had become more aware of social injustice and its prevalence in the lives of others, and that this awareness had helped them be more compassionate. Some of the men explicitly made reference to "the earth" as a focal point for expressing justice and compassion.

Sense of Vocation, Mission, or Purpose in Life. Although there was some repetition between the answers given in response to the other questions and this question, it was valuable to discover how the participants reflected on vocation when they were given an opportunity to do so in a systematic and self-conscious way. Even freshmen and sophomores had relatively sophisticated understandings of the concept of vocation. None of the students thought that vocation pertained exclusively to a calling to priesthood or another professional vocation. Almost all of them viewed vocation as something more than a job or career. Men in senior groups frequently referred to how their involvement in the group had helped them align their priorities in a proper way. Although the men professed refined notions *about* vocation at all levels of their college careers, few believed they had yet fully discovered their personal vocations. Most of them said they would require greater experience in life in order to understand their vocations. Seniors emphasized how their development of life skills (listening without judgment, sharing, helping others) helped them focus their lives, and the men in these groups acknowledged that questions about vocation had surfaced for them through their discussion in the groups on issues that ranged from one man explaining how he viewed working with the homeless through a Catholic Charities program as a way to help other men to another man who was facing a tour of duty in the army, which he regarded as a call to service, realizing that the question he would now have to answer was a basic ethical one: Can I kill someone?

Adapting the Saint John's Model to Other Contexts

Longwood and Muesse concluded that the spirituality groups program at Saint John's has been highly successful in assisting college men in breaking down masculine stereotypes, enriching their relationships with others, enhancing their spiritual development, and deepening their understanding of their vocations. Particular factors contributed to the success of the Saint John's men's spirituality program: a mission statement that is explicit in its commitment to critical examination of gender, a community of monks and other university staff who were willing to reflect on their spiritual autobiographies and assist young men in their spiritual development, the Benedictine tradition as a rich resource for challenging the limitations of prevailing notions of masculinity, and leadership in the Office of Student Development that was willing to take the risk and dedicate resources to this creative experiment.

Although it is unlikely that other institutions would be able to duplicate Saint John's model, we believe it is possible to adapt it to other institutional settings. Adaptation requires careful attention to the particular institutional cultures within which the programs are initiated. Those who wish to cultivate such programs ought to take into account a number of considerations.

First, a spirituality program should be established on clear foundations. If the institution has a mission statement, it should be carefully evaluated to determine if and how it might provide a framework of values that could inform the development of such a program. People working in institutions that are self-consciously related to spiritual traditions should explore how the resources within those traditions might be interpreted to help students explore their own spirituality without insisting upon a particular normative spirituality that the students would be expected to adopt. For example, can the values of a Presbyterian institution be construed in such a way as to encourage the spiritual development of students who are not Presbyterian, or even Christian? Within secular institutions or other institutions that do not have mission statements that could serve as a foundation for a spirituality program, campus ministries might take the initiative in program development.

Second, a crucial element of a successful program will be identification of a mentoring community from which group facilitators can be drawn, beginning perhaps with faculty and staff of the university. In choosing people to serve as group facilitators, it is important to select individuals who are themselves willing to examine their own spiritual autobiographies and to deconstruct the male gender role for themselves in order to assist young men to do this in their own lives.

Several elements will be important in successful management of the program. There should be an administrator to oversee the program, to arrange for a process to select participants, to provide support for facilitators of the group, and to monitor the changing needs of those involved in the program. The facilitators should have opportunities to continue to be nurtured in their own spiritual development, perhaps through periodic meetings with each other, retreats, or other forums. It is wise to begin with a modest-sized program, perhaps starting with one or two groups, and if it becomes apparent that there is interest in broadening the program it can gradually be expanded. Those administering and facilitating groups are encouraged to consult the broad range of resources relevant to men's lives and collegiate spirituality. Websites maintained by organizations such as the American Men's Studies Association (http://mensstudies.org) and the Center for the Study of Values in College Student Development (http://www.collegevalues.org) are excellent places to begin.

When a group is formed, it is important that all participants regard it as a community in which it is safe to explore deep personal issues in a supportive and nonjudgmental atmosphere. At the outset, the facilitators should explain the importance of confidentiality, commitment, and communication. If these elements are firmly established, group members will come to regard each other as a covenanted community and their meetings as sacred time.

Groups should be encouraged to regard meetings as a time to explore members' inner lives and important relationships, not as a forum to discuss abstract ideas. A lecture or a book discussion may be useful as a way to stimulate interest in such a group, but groups should quickly move beyond this more academic framework. Once a group is formed, the facilitators should encourage participants to use *I* statements as they share their experiences and respond to others.

The Benefits of the Program

A lively spirituality group program can impart significant benefits to institutions of higher education. It can furnish a cutting-edge opportunity to contribute to the holistic development of men in the collegiate environment. Such groups are a way to respond to students' needs for opportunities to attend to the spiritual dimensions of their lives and can help them challenge restrictions imposed by traditional masculinity. As institutions of higher education encounter increasing cultural, ethnic, and religious diversity among their students, a spirituality group program can be an effective means of community building, fostering a safe environment to explore and appreciate differences. A spirituality group program can create opportunities for students to interact with faculty and staff to develop relationships that enable them to feel more at home in the institutions, since most students leave behind networks of support they had in high school when they enter college.

We believe that the development of men's spirituality programs, appropriately adapted to draw upon the resources and to meet the needs of the men on the campuses in which they are implemented, can be an important way in which men can connect more fully to themselves and to other men. They can be one means, among others, to contribute to the holistic development of men, enabling them to be more integrated within themselves and in their relationships with others.

References

Bennett, J. "Spirituality and the Vitality of Academic Life." *Journal of College and Character*, vol. 2, 2004. http://www.collegevalues.org/articles.cfm. Access date: March 23, 2004.

Chickering, A. "Encouraging Authenticity and Spirituality in Higher Education." *Journal of College and Character*, vol. 2, 2004, 2. http://www.collegevalues.org/articles.cfm. Access date: March 23, 2004.

Herndon, M. K. "Expressions of Spirituality Among African-American College Males." *Journal of Men's Studies*, 2003, 12(1), 75–84.

Kirkley, E. A. "Is It Manly to Be Christian?: The Debate in Victorian and Modern America." In S. B. Boyd, W. M. Longwood, and M. W. Muesse (eds.), *Redeeming Men: Religion and Masculinities*. Louisville, Ky.: Westminster John Knox Press, 1996.

Miller, V. M., Ryan, M. M., and Laurence, P. L. (eds.). *Transforming Campus Life: Reflections on Spirituality and Religious Pluralism*. New York: Lang, 2001.

Sax, L. "Citizenship and Spirituality Among College Students: What Have We Learned and Where Are We Headed?" *Journal of College and Character*, vol. 2, 2004. http://www.collegevalues.org/articles.cfm. Access date: March 23, 2004.

Young, J. R. "Survey Finds Spiritual Leanings Among Most College Students." *Chronicle of Higher Education*, Nov. 28, 2003, p. A36.

W. MERLE LONGWOOD *is professor of religious studies at Siena College in Loudonville, New York.*

MARK W. MUESSE *is associate professor of religious studies at Rhodes College in Memphis, Tennessee.*

WILLIAM C. SCHIPPER, O.S.B., *is a member of Saint John's Abbey and faculty resident at Saint John's University in Collegeville, Minnesota, and a Ph.D. candidate in men's studies at Union Institute and University in Cincinnati, Ohio.*

Afterword

Michael Kimmel

That there is a "crisis" concerning men in higher education these days has become almost a journalistic commonplace. A dramatic decline in enrollments relative to women; an equally dramatic convergence in test scores, especially in the sciences; and the daily barrage of accounts of sexual assault, harassment, violence, and other behavioral problems add up to an apparently serious social problem.

For example, we read that women now constitute the majority of students on college campuses, passing men in 1982, such that in eight years women will earn 58 percent of bachelor's degrees in U.S. colleges. One reporter, obviously a terrible statistics student, tells us that if present trends continue, "the graduation line in 2068 will be all females." (That's like saying that because the black enrollment at Ol' Miss was 1 in 1964, 350 in 1970, and 4,000 in 1980, that sometime around 1994 there were no white students there.) Doomsayers lament that women now outnumber men in the social and behavioral sciences by about three to one, and how they've invaded such traditionally male bastions as engineering (where they now make up 20 percent) and biology and business (virtually par; see Koerner, 1999; and Lewin, 1998).

They are also doing worse and worse: women now earn the overwhelming majority of campus academic honors, participate in extracurricular activities, and do better on standardized tests than men. And they're catching up in athletic participation—the last holdout of male numerical supremacy.

So it seemed logical that the title of the conference that gave birth to this issue of *New Directions for Student Services* was Reconnecting Males to Higher Education. But when, exactly, had males disconnected? Who disconnected them?

It turns out that the evidence for this crisis is spotty at best. The presumed causes turn out not to hold up empirically at all.

For one thing, there is no decrease in male enrollment in higher education. More *people* are going to college than ever before. Although the rate of increase in enrollment is higher for women than it is for men, more men are going to college than ever. Although feminist educational reforms have undoubtedly enabled more girls to pursue careers in, for example, the sciences, these reforms—attention to individual learning styles, flexibility in educational methodologies, new classroom configurations, and increased teacher training—have also undoubtedly benefited boys as well.

The crisis of males in higher education has to do with masculinities—with both the multiple definitions of masculinity articulated by different groups of men and the intersections of gender relations with other lines of identity and inequality, such as race, class, ethnicity, and sexuality.

It is the great virtue of this collection that it begins where the questions at that conference left off. The authors here do not accept a facile biological essentialism that *males* are in crisis but instead are aware that different groups of men are experiencing this crisis quite differently.

For example, in Chapter One, Obie Clayton, Cynthia Lucas Hewitt, and Eddie Gaffney together explode the myth that "males" are experiencing a crisis, but they are insistent that lower-income men and men of color are at increased risk in higher education today. The numbers are startling. According to the U.S. Department of Education, the gender distribution of middle-class white students is even: 50 percent of all middle-class white students are male, and 50 percent are female. Not much of a crisis of male enrollments there!

But 68 percent of all lower-income black students in college are female. Only 43 percent of lower-income Hispanic students are male. (Ironically, upper-income Hispanics are exactly fifty-fifty in their gender ratio, while only 41 percent of upper-class black students are male.) It turns out that what has been trumpeted as a gender crisis may actually have more to do with class and race.

If the crisis among men is a crisis of *some* men, this requires that we raise other questions and search for other causes for the crisis of males than feminist educational reforms designed to enhance the enrollment and achievement of women. For how could these reforms have such dramatically different impacts on black and Latino males from the impact on middle-class white men? Are men of color more "vulnerable" to feminist reforms than white men?

As Rocco Capraro insists, the problem of males in higher education is a problem that is well addressed by "men's studies," that academic offshoot of women's studies that takes men and masculinities as its object of study. Capraro understands that the issue is less about males and more about gender—that is, any discussion of the problems that men might be experiencing has more to do with ideologies of masculinity than it does with testosterone or Y chromosomes.

As Cynthia Spence and Manju Parikh remind us in Chapter Three, to raise the issue of masculinity means to make *gender* visible. For that project, our greatest ally is the efforts of feminist scholars to make gender visible within the context of women's experiences. Women's studies did far more than make women the object of analysis and the center of intellectual inquiry. Women's studies also provided a theoretical apparatus, a framework through which to view gender relations, as well as a methodology by which one can interrogate the meanings of femininity and the structure of those gender relations.

As a result, they argue, men's studies must remain consistent with the insights and perspectives of women's studies. This doesn't just mean that men's scholars must do their homework and familiarize themselves with the rich literature created by women's studies scholars—though they must do that. Nor could it possibly mean facile and formulaic application of theories and methods of women's studies applied to men's lives without an appreciation of the specificity of men's lives—in all their variations and richness as well.

In fact, we might go further and suggest that the insights of African American studies, Latino studies, Ethnic studies, and gay and lesbian studies also have some important perspectives that can shed new light from different angles on men's experiences. (It is an unfortunate irony that the discussion of the multiplicity of masculinities in this volume contains virtually no mention of gay men, either on campus or off.)

The remaining four chapters—on student affairs programming (by Tracy Davis and Jason Laker), on health (by Will Courtenay), about emotional and psychological development (by Randall Ludeman), and on spirituality (by Merle Longwood, Mark Muesse, and William Schipper)—take up the challenge posed by the first three chapters. They represent a second part of the volume in which administrators and academics concerned with student affairs issues apply the perspectives articulated by the writers in the first part. In this way, the volume sustains a coherent internal organization, presenting theory and then practice.

These chapters don't link up interrogations about masculinities to specific political problem areas, such as violence, but rather elaborate various aspects of masculinity, such as health and spirituality. Taken together, they suggest an important formula for engaging men on college campuses: the imperative that men be engaged *as men,* and not simply as males. That is to say, engagement must come through a confrontation with masculinities, with gender and its attendant ideologies, and in its relations to women and to other men.

Engaging men-as-men is the exact opposite of "boys will be boys"—the four most depressing words in educational policy circles these days. What "boys will be boys" usually means is a sigh of abject resignation (or, even worse, unapologetic celebration) that boys are simply who they are and who they are is violent, aggressive, rapacious predators. Wired by brain chemistry and propelled by testosterone, "boys will be boys" means that they are ultimately incorrigible—unchanging, eternally violent, and out of control.

By contrast, feminist inquiries and men's studies scholars believe that men can do far better than that, that men are far more honorable than such "male bashing" assumptions that all males are biologically driven to be such rapacious predators. But the only way to get there is to engage with men about gender.

The last chapter, which examines a spirituality group at Saint John's University, is a good example of how engaging men-as-men, within a context of spiritual inquiry, can be a transformative experience for a variety of men. Saint John's is certainly a college *of* men; it is an all-male institution associated with an all-female college, the nearby College of Saint Benedict. As a Benedictine institution, it is certainly a college *by* men; it is administered by monks with a secular and clerical staff, with a monastery attached to the campus, and a magnificent modern chapel as the campus's geographic and moral center.

But, the authors imply, until the monks and priests and faculty and students began a men's group within the college, Saint John's wasn't really a college *for* men. To be sure, the university's staff and administration believed that they were developing programs for men, but such programs did not engage questions of gender and masculinity.

To be a college *for* men requires an engagement not only with the males of the species but also with the thoughts such creatures have rolling around in their heads about the meaning of that anatomy. To engage men in higher education requires that we begin to think about how to integrate masculinities into the collegiate experience of men—in the classroom, in extracurricular programming, in residential life. Gender saturates our intellectual, emotional, physical, and spiritual experiences, and any college that seeks to engage (or reconnect) men to higher education would do well to begin with engaging men—as men.

References

Koerner, B. "Where the Boys Aren't." *U.S. News and World Report,* Feb. 8, 1999, pp. 46–52.
Lewin, T. "American Colleges Begin to Ask, Where Have All the Men Gone?" *New York Times,* Dec. 6, 1998.

MICHAEL KIMMEL *is professor in the Department of Sociology at the State University of New York at Stony Brook.*

INDEX

Academic affairs programs, male students' lack of engagement in, 47
Academic time commitment, gender gap in, 3
Accreditation agencies, accountability of, 20–21
Adams, R., 24
Alcohol abuse, 48, 60; interventions, 30–31, 71; and male behavioral problems, 77; and male violence, 76
American College Personnel Association (ACPA), 49; Standing Committee for Men, 5
American Council on Education (ACE), 49
Arendell, T., 24
At-risk behaviors: gender gap in, 59, 60; health interventions for, 70–71; and judicial process, 82; and psychology of brotherhood, 28
At-risk male education, 98; policy development and recommendations, 19–20; national action agenda for, 20–21
August, E. R., 24
Automobile accidents, male risk from, 65–66

Belsie, L., 4
Bennett, J., 88
Berkowitz, A., 24, 28, 31, 70, 76
Billson, J. M., 24
Black administrators, 15
Black male education: barriers to, 12–18; and development of "soft skills," 40; and disenfranchisement of African Americans, 40; and institutional racism, 12; as political/civil rights issue, 15–16; prevalence of, 10, 11–12; in single-sex schools, 14
Black male teachers: and cultural congruence, 14–15; statistics on, 15
Black male youth: academic attitudes of, 13–14; drug offenses of, 17–18; and family finances, 17; gender identities of, 13–14; incarceration of, 17; subcultures, 13, 16–17; suspension/expulsion of, 17–18
Blazina, C., 79

Blumenson, E., 15, 17, 18
Boca Zinn, M., 43
Bostic, D., 83
Boyd, S. B., 6
Brannon, R., 25
Brittan, A., 26
Brod, H., 24, 26, 50
Brody, L. R., 53
Brooks, G. R., 76
Brown, R., 78
Bryk, A. S., 18
Byrd, R., 39

Campus Compact Annual Service Statistics, 3
Capraro, R. L., 23, 24, 25, 27, 28, 30, 47, 79
Carter, C. A., 70
Chickering, A. W., 79, 81, 88
Clatterbaugh, K., 25
Cochran, S. V., 78, 79
Coldwell, L., 48
College career centers, men's use of, 3
College education, relevance of, 10
College of Saint Benedict, collaborative gender and women's studies minor at, 41–44
College enrollment, gender gap in, 9, 10–11, 97
Combs, A., 13
Conlin, M., 1
Connell, R. W., 26
Cournoyer, R. J., 79
Courtenay, W. H., 3, 24, 59, 60, 61, 62, 63, 64, 65, 66, 67, 68, 69, 76, 79
Creamer, G. D., 77

Dannells, M. D., 77, 78, 81
Dartmouth College Men's Project, 54–55
David, D. S., 25
Davis, T. L., 50, 51, 52
Depression, male behavioral responses to, 66
Deutsch, C., 77
DeVore, D., 82
Diamond, J., 76
DiClemente, C., 69
Dill, B. T., 43

Dowdall, G., 77
Drug Free Student Loans Act, 18

Earnings: and purchasing power, 17; of recent male high school graduates, 17
Educational outcomes: gender gap in, 1; race and class disparities in, 9
England, R. E., 15
Engs, R. C., 77

Fagot, B., 78
Faludi, S., 27
Farrell, W., 48
Federal Bureau of Investigation, 76
Feminist educational reforms, male benefits from, 97
Feminist theory, essentialist assumptions in, 43
Filene, P. G., 25
Financial aid, and drug offenses, 17
Foster, M., 15
Foucault, M., 81
Friedan, B., 24

Gallagher, R. P., 77
Garbarino, J., 27
Gehring, D. D., 81
Gender and women's studies minor, 41–44; feminism and, 43; and men's gender concerns, 42, 43; and women's oppression, 43–44
Gender awareness education, 5
Gender identity, and male role set, 13–14
Gentilcore, K., 82
Gereffi, G., 17
Gerzon, M., 24
Gilligan, C., 40
Gilmore, D. D., 24
Gold, J., 28
Gonzalez, G., 83
Good, G. E., 51, 76
Greenberg, B., 78
Guy-Sheftall, B., 39

Hacker, A., 1
Hall, J. A., 65
Hanson, D. J., 77
Harmon, W. W., 77
Harrington, N. G., 71
Hartley, R., 78
Health behaviors: gender gap in, 59–60; high-risk, 48, 60; and male socialization, 61; media's impact on, 61–62;

and traditional attitudes toward masculinity, 60
Health interventions: clinical practice guideline for, 62–68; and diagnosis, 66; education and counseling in, 64–65; evidence-based strategies in, 68–69, 70; gender-specific, 69, 70; and male motivation/compliance, 67–68; and maintenance of health, 67; and men's body image, 64; and men's perceived invulnerability, 65–66; and risky behaviors, 70–71; and sexual concerns, 64; and support systems, 66–67; transtheoretical model for, 69–70; validation and normalization of concerns in, 63–64
Hearn, J., 24
Helmreich, R., 52
Helms, J. E., 53
Hepper, M., 76
Heppner, P. P., 79
Herndon, M. K., 88
Higher Education Research Institute (HERI), 6
Hillenbrand-Gunn, T., 76
Hine, D. C., 24
Homophobia: and concept of masculinity, 38; strategies for dealing with, 52
Hong, L., 76, 77
Hughes, G., 43
Hyde, J., 78

Irvine, J., 15

Jenkins, E., 24
Jensen, R., 44
Jiobu, R. M., 12
Job market, and male college decisions, 16
Johnson, A., 44
Jones, S. R., 52
Judicial program(s): and educational sanctions, 80; group process in, 83; philosophy and process, 81–82; and male emotionality, 82; mediation venue in, 82; research, 77–78; restorative justice model of, 82; and students' developmental needs, 80–81

Kahnweiler, W. M., 70
Kaufman, M., 26, 50
Keating, L. A., 49
Keeling, R. P., 59, 70
Kegan, R., 53
Kellom, G., 1

Kilmartin, C., 44
Kilmer, J. R., 28
Kimmel, M., 24, 27, 37, 38, 47, 50
King, J. E., 10, 11
King, P. M., 48
Kirkley, E. A., 87
Koerner, B., 97
Krugman, S., 28

Laker, J., 53
Lancer, J., 15
Lather, P., 81, 84
Laurence, P. L., 88
Leadership programs, and visible skills, 39
Lee, V. E., 18
Levant, R. F., 78, 79
Levin, B., 76
Levinson, D. J., 24, 79
Lewin, T., 97
Liberal arts education, male participation in, 11, 13–14
Liddell, D. L., 51
Life expectancy, gender gap in, 3
Lingenfelter, C. O., 77
Linn, M., 78
Longwood, W. M., 6
Lower-income youth education: barriers to, 12–13, 17; gender gap in, 10, 11, 98; and war on drugs, 17–18
Lykes, M. D., 79
Lyman, P., 28

Mahalik, J. R., 79
Maher, F. A., 36
Majors, R., 24
Male education: and choice of discipline, 13–14; cost-benefit analysis of, 16–17; crisis, myth of, 1, 97–98; and employment prospects, 16; and identity consumption, 16–17; and physical activities, 14
Male employment, and nature of job market, 16
Male gender role conflict, theory of, 79
Male misconduct, 75–84; and gender role socialization, 76, 77–80; institutional interventions for, 77–78, 80–83; and judicial programs, 80–83; profile of offenders, 77; and substance abuse, 48, 60, 77; and traditional hegemonic male norms, 76
Male socialization, 77–80; characteristics of, 50; conceptual base for, 50; emotional repression in, 78–79; fear of femininity instilled in, 79; health effects of, 61; and "manliness" versus "domesticity" tensions, 27–29; and self-destructive behavior, 76, 77; and traditional masculine code, 78
Male spirituality, 87–100; academic institutions' neglect of, 88; and concept of vocation, 92; and dominant masculine values, 61, 65, 87–88
Male students, facilitating discussions with, 57
Male violence: generalizations about, 43–44; and role socialization, 76; and psychopathology, 77
Male youth culture: black, 13, 16–17; high-risk behaviors in, 28, 60; and transition to manhood, 27–28
Marks, H., 18
Marshall, D., 76
Masculinity concepts: in developmental theory, 50–51; and health attitudes, 60; of multiple masculinities, 51–52; and paradoxical nature of masculinity, 26–27; and programs/services for men, 29; and sex role strain paradigm, 25–26; and social stratification, 14; spirituality and, 87–88; stereotypes in, 61, 65; traditional, and gender-role conflict, 50
Masculinity studies, 14. See also Men's studies
Massey, W. E., 1
McCarthy, R., 11
McCreary, D. R., 3, 60, 64
McEwen, M. K., 52
Meier, K. J., 15
"Men on Our Campuses," 11, 14, 15, 17, 29
Men's movement, diverse goals in, 25
Men's spirituality groups: benefits of, 90–92; facilitators and administrators of, 93–94; formation and format of, 89–90; institutional benefits of, 94; and institutional cultures, 93; and relationship effects, 91; themes in, 90
Men's studies, 2, 23–31, 39, 83–84; concept of masculinities in, 26, 29; defined, 23–24; foundational texts, 25; integrated with women's studies, 41–44; male-centered pedagogy in, 36–37; representative topics in, 24; theory and history of, 25–29; value orientation of, 24; and women's oppression, 25; and women's studies, 24, 98–99

Merighi, J. R., 3, 60
Messner, M. A., 24, 47, 50
Meth, R. L., 49, 79
Middle–class white students, gender distribution of, 98
Mies, M., 17
Miller, M., 28
Miller, V. M., 88
Minority teachers, positive impacts of, 14–15
Monette, P., 24
Morehouse College, 1, 9; founding of, 35; leadership development model (Morehouse Man), 36, 37, 39; theme of racial uplift in, 36, 40–41. *See also* Single-sex male institutions
Morman, M. T., 69
Mortality, gender gap in, 59
Mortenson, T., 17
Muesse, W. M., 6
Multiple Dimensions of Identity (MDI) model, 52
Murray, N., 3

Nakagawa, K., 16
Nathanson, C. A., 79
National Association for Single-Sex Public Education, 18
National Center for Injury Prevention and Control, 48
Native American college enrollment, gender gap in, 10
Nelson, J., 88
Neururer, J., 28
Nilsen, E. S., 15, 17, 18
Norcross, J., 69
Nuwer, H., 28
Nyland, D. and D., 49

Oliver, M. L., 17
O'Neil, J., 50–53
O'Neil, J. M., 79
Onishi, N., 12
Osborne, J. W., 13
Owen, S., 50

Parikh, 5, 30, 35, 41
Parsons, T., 13
Pasick, R. S., 49
Patrick, M. S., 62
Peele, T., 15
Perkins, H. W., 28
Physical activity: male need for, 14; and men's expressiveness, 51

Pierce College (Washington) men's programs, 54
Pleck, J., 25, 26
Polite, V. C., 13
Pollack, W., 24, 27, 47, 51, 52, 53, 76, 78
Prevention programs for men: alcohol-related, 30–31; critical features of, 30–31; and male intimacy issues, 31; men's studies pedagogy in, 31; on sexual violence, 31
Prochaska, J., 69
Pronger, B., 24

Rabinowitz, F. E., 78, 79
Racism, and educational access, 12
Reconnecting Males to Liberal Education symposium, 9
Reich, R., 16
Reio, T. G., 48
Reisser, L., 79
Rhoads, R. A., 76, 79
Riordan, C., 18
Roter, D. L., 65
Rothstein, R., 16
Rotundo, E. A., 27, 28
Ryan, M. M., 88

Saint John's University, 99–100; Center for Men's Leadership and Service, 54; collaborative gender and women's studies minor at, 41–44; men's spirituality groups at, 88–93
Sanday, P., 76
Sassen, S., 16
Saucier, D. M., 64
Savran, D., 24
Sax, L., 3, 88
Scher, M., 50
Schweigert, F. J., 82
Seidler, V., 76
Sensation seekers, health interventions for, 70–71
Serr, R. L., 82
Service programs, male versus female participation in, 3
Sexual assault prevention program, 31
Shame theory, 28
Shapiro, T. M., 17
Sharpe, M. J., 79
Silverstein, L. B., 76
Single-sex male education: beneficial effects of, 18; of black men, 14, 18; educational perspective in, 18; and

homophobia, 45n5; and male-centered pedagogy, 36–37; masculinity/self–definition issues and, 37–38; and narratives of masculinity/male leadership, 41; in public schools, 18–19; and sexual discrimination, 18–19; women's college perspective on, 36–37, 38. *See also* Morehouse College; Saint John's University
Six-Point HEALTH Plan, 62–68
Slaughter-Defoe, D., 15
Smith, D. E., 80
Smitherman, G., 15, 18
Sommers, C. H., 27
Spelman College, 35, 36
Spence, J. T., 30, 52
Stanton, A. L., 60, 62
Stewart, A. J., 79
Stewart, J., Jr., 15
Stillson, R., 50
Stuber, D., 77
Student affairs services, 47–55; and alliances with men's studies, 29–30; case examples of, 54–55; and developmental interventions, 52–53; framework for design of, 49–53; gender role conflict theoretical framework for, 50–51; men's rejection/lack of engagement in, 29, 47; and multiple masculinities, 51–52; and prevention programs, 30–31; professional socialization process and, 48–49; required, 31
Study abroad, male versus female, 3
Study habits, gender gap in, 2–3
Suicide, male, 3, 48, 66

Taber, R. S., 82
Testicular self-examination, 65, 68–69
Thompson Tetreault, M. K., 36
Title IX of the Civil Rights Acts, 19
Tucker, C. M., 13

U.S. Census Bureau, 10
U.S. Commission on Civil Rights, 12
U.S. Department of Education, 11, 15
U.S. Department of Health and Human Services (DHHS), 59, 66, 76
U.S. Department of Labor, 11

Valois, R., 76
Van Kuren, N. F., 77
Voting patterns, gender gap in, 3–4

Wang, L., 76
Warters, W. C., 82
Watkins, C. E., 79
Watson, C., 15, 18
Wechsler, H., 28, 77
Willis, P., 14
Wisniewski, N., 76
Witherell, S., 3
Women's studies, and men's gender concerns, 42–43, 98–99
Wood, P. K., 51

Young, J., 6
Young, R., 48, 88

Zuckerman, M., 70

Back Issue/Subscription Order Form

Copy or detach and send to:
Jossey-Bass, A Wiley Imprint, 989 Market Street, San Francisco CA, 94103-1741

Call or fax toll-free: Phone 888-378-2537 6:30AM – 3PM PST; Fax 888-481-2665

Back Issues: Please send me the following issues at $27 each
(Important: please include ISBN number with your order.)

_____

_____

_____

$ _____   Total for single issues

$ _____   SHIPPING CHARGES: SURFACE   Domestic Canadian

First Item	$5.00	$6.00
Each Add'l Item	$3.00	$1.50

For next-day and second-day delivery rates, call the number listed above.

Subscriptions   Please __ start __ renew my subscription to *New Directions for Student Services* for the year 2_____ at the following rate:

U.S.	__ Individual $75	__ Institutional $170
Canada	__ Individual $75	__ Institutional $210
All Others	__ Individual $99	__ Institutional $244
U.S. Online Subscription		__ Institutional $170
U.S. Print & Online Subscription		__ Institutional $187

**For more information about online subscriptions visit
www.wileyinterscience.com**

$ _____ Total single issues and subscriptions (Add appropriate sales tax for your state for single issue orders. No sales tax for U.S. subscriptions. Canadian residents, add GST for subscriptions and single issues.)

__Payment enclosed (U.S. check or money order only)
__VISA __ MC __ AmEx Card #_____Exp.Date_____

Signature _____Day Phone_____

__Bill Me (U.S. institutional orders only. Purchase order required.)

Purchase order # _____
      Federal Tax ID13559302   **GST 89102 8052**

Name _____

Address _____

_____

Phone _____ E-mail _____

For more information about Jossey-Bass, visit our Web site at www.josseybass.com

OTHER TITLES AVAILABLE IN THE
New Directions for Student Services Series
JOHN H. SCHUH, EDITOR-IN-CHIEF
ELIZABETH J. WHITT, ASSOCIATE EDITOR

SS106   **Serving the Millennial Generation**
         Michael D. Coomes, Robert DeBard
         Focuses on the next enrollment boom, students born after 1981, known as
         the Millennial generation. Examines these students' attitudes, beliefs, and
         behaviors, and makes recommendations to student affairs practitioners for
         working with them. Discusses historical and cultural influences that shape
         generations, demographics, teaching and learning patterns of Millennials,
         and how student affairs can best educate and serve them.
         ISBN: 0-7879-7606-7

SS105   **Addressing the Unique Needs of Latino American Students**
         Anna M. Ortiz
         Explores the experiences of the fast-growing population of Latinos in higher
         education, and what these students need from student affairs. This volume
         examines the influence of the Latino family, socioeconomic levels, cultural
         barriers, and other factors to understand the challenges faced by Latinos.
         Discusses administration, student groups, community colleges, support
         programs, cultural identity, Hispanic-Serving Institutions, and more.
         ISBN: 0-7879-7479-X

SS104   **Meeting the Needs of African American Women**
         Mary F. Howard-Hamilton
         Identifies and explores the critical needs for African American women as
         students, faculty, and administrators. This volume introduces theoretical
         frameworks and practical applications for addressing challenges; discusses
         identity and spirituality; explores the importance of programming support in
         recruitment and retention; describes the benefits of mentoring; and provides
         illuminating case studies of black women's issues in higher education.
         ISBN: 0-7879-7280-0

SS103   **Contemporary Financial Issues in Student Affairs**
         John H. Schuh
         This volume addresses the challenging financial situation facing higher
         education and offers creative solutions for student affairs staff. Topics
         include the differences between public and private institutions in funding
         student activities, how to demonstrate financial accountability to
         stakeholders, plus ways to address budget challenges in student unions,
         health centers, campus recreation, counseling centers, and student housing.
         ISBN: 0-7879-7173-1

SS102   **Meeting the Special Needs of Adult Students**
         Deborah Kilgore, Penny J. Rice
         This volume examines the ways student services professionals can best help
         adult learners. Chapters highlight the specific challenges that adult
         enrollment brings to traditional four-year and postgraduate institutions,
         which are often focused on the traditional-aged student experience.
         Explaining that adult students are typically involved in campus life in
         different ways than younger students are, the volume provides student
         services professionals with good guidance on serving an ever-growing
         population.
         ISBN: 0-7879-6991-5

NEW DIRECTIONS FOR STUDENT SERVICES
IS NOW AVAILABLE ONLINE AT WILEY INTERSCIENCE

What is Wiley InterScience?

Wiley InterScience is the dynamic online content service from John Wiley & Sons delivering the full text of over 300 leading scientific, technical, medical, and professional journals, plus major reference works, the acclaimed *Current Protocols* laboratory manuals, and even the full text of select Wiley print books online.

What are some special features of Wiley InterScience?

Wiley InterScience Alerts is a service that delivers table of contents via e-mail for any journal available on Wiley InterScience as soon as a new issue is published online.
Early View is Wiley's exclusive service presenting individual articles online as soon as they are ready, even before the release of the compiled print issue. These articles are complete, peer-reviewed, and citable.
CrossRef is the innovative multi-publisher reference linking system enabling readers to move seamlessly from a reference in a journal article to the cited publication, typically located on a different server and published by a different publisher.

How can I access Wiley InterScience?

Visit http://www.interscience.wiley.com

Guest Users can browse Wiley InterScience for unrestricted access to journal Tables of Contents and Article Abstracts, or use the powerful search engine.
Registered Users are provided with a *Personal Home Page* to store and manage customized alerts, searches, and links to favorite journals and articles. Additionally, Registered Users can view free Online Sample Issues and preview selected material from major reference works.
Licensed Customers are entitled to access full-text journal articles in PDF, with select journals also offering full-text HTML.

How do I become an Authorized User?

Authorized Users are individuals authorized by a paying Customer to have access to the journals in Wiley InterScience. For example, a university that subscribes to Wiley journals is considered to be the Customer. Faculty, staff and students authorized by the university to have access to those journals in Wiley InterScience are Authorized Users. Users should contact their Library for information on which Wiley journals they have access to in Wiley InterScience.

ASK YOUR INSTITUTION ABOUT WILEY INTERSCIENCE TODAY!